The Big Little School

OTHER BOOKS BY ROBERT W. LYNN

Protestant Strategies in Education.

OTHER BOOKS BY ELLIOTT WRIGHT

Black Manifesto: Religion, Racism and Reparations
Can these Bones Live?
The Challenge of Mission
At the Edge of Hope: Christian Laity in Paradox
Go Free

The Big Little School

Two Hundred Years of the Sunday School

second edition revised and enlarged

ROBERT W. LYNN AND ELLIOTT WRIGHT

Religious Education Press
Birmingham, Alabama

Abingdon
Nashville, Tennessee

Library of Congress Cataloging in Publication Data

Lynn, Robert W
  The big little school.

  Includes bibliographical references and index.
    1. Sunday-schools—United States—History.
I. Wright, H. Elliott, 1937–   joint author.
II. Title
BV1516.A1L9 1980   268'.0973   79-27864

Religious Education Press
ISBN 0-89135-021-7

Abingdon
ISBN 1-687-03523-6

Religious Education Press, Inc.   Abingdon
1531 Wellington Road   201 Eighth Avenue South
Birmingham, Alabama 35209   Nashville, Tennessee 37202

Contents

v

Foreword

"The Sunday school is dying." "It is dead!" "Let's bury it and start anew!" The funeral orations have been preached for many years. A national magazine once labeled it "the most wasted hour of the week." But the Sunday school refuses to die. There is scarcely a church in the country without a Sunday Church School. New churches are still being built with the Sunday school as the forerunner for gathering the new congregations. There are extremely large Sunday schools with thousands of members, and small Sunday schools struggling to keep going. But they do, led by dedicated, caring persons who believe that the Sunday setting is an appropriate and meaningful time for carrying on at least a part of the church's educational ministry. So, for the Sunday school, it is not actually a question of "to be or not to be." The Sunday school is. It exists, and has no intention of folding up or dying.

The calls for "alternatives" to the Sunday school which are sounded continually, mostly by professional Christian educators rather than local practioners, should not go unheeded. For although the one or two hour sessions on a

1

Sunday are not enough, the value is not dependent on the day of the week, or the length, but on what actually takes place at that time, on the interactions between persons who are learning together in the faith community on *Sundays.*

The history of the Sunday school movement is an interesting one, filled with bits of legend, humor, pathos, and sometimes controversy. But always we are impressed with the dedication and zeal of the early pioneers of the movement, most of them lay persons, who persevered often in the face of official ecclesiastical opposition. The gallery of the "saints of the movement" includes an impressive list of famous names and personalities, but there were also the many hundreds of humble, dedicated, unsung co-workers whose names are lost in history, but to whom we owe a multitude of debt and gratitude.

These early pioneers worked for the "cause" without serious regard for denominational affiliation. The early Sunday schools were called undenominational or nondenominational. The nondenominational nature of the early Sunday School work made it a natural for the formation of Sunday School Associations on an interdenominational basis. These Sunday School Associations became the forerunners of the Conciliar movement in the United States. The Councils of Churches, or present day Ecumenical Agencies, grew out of the early Sunday School Associations or Christian Education Councils. Through a strange quirk of history, or a denial of their historical roots, these same Councils or local and regional ecumenical agencies have largely abandoned Christian education work as a major interdenominational area of concern. They have tended to focus largely on more current social issues rather than the ongoing concern for Christian nurture. This may not be the fault of the conciliar movement itself, but may indicate the shift in denominational priorities, the choice of working on Christian education programs through their own judicatories rather than cooperatively. When the denominations took over the Sunday school and claimed it as their own, it became known as the Sunday Church School, or the church school on Sundays. In the same way, denominations appropriated other forms of educational ministry begun as nondenominational enterprises and incorporated them as part of their comprehensive church school model. For example, the impetus for the denominational youth fellowships grew out of the success of the nondenominational youth movement known as Christian Endeavor founded in 1881.

In the early 1900s, the Daily Vacation Bible School movement was started in New York City by an executive of the Baptist Mission Society with a concern for children idle during the summer months. The movement soon became a department of the New York Federation of Churches. Later it was taken over by the denominations, renamed the Vacation Church School, becoming another setting for the denominational comprehensive church school. Although many Vacation Church Schools today remain cooperative community programs, curriculum resources are published cooperatively as well as denominationally, and also independently, allowing local churches a variety of resource options.

In 1914, the Weekday Religious Education movement was started by a superintendent of schools in Gary, Indiana. Although it began as a denominational effort, almost immediately it was deemed wiser to make it interdenominational, a cooperative effort, and it has largely remained so. The early program included four areas: study, work, play, and religion. Since Superintendent Wirt was aware of the problems of separation of church and state, he called upon the churches to provide the religious instruction. The movement was taken over by Councils of Churches or Ministerial Associations and spread rapidly throughout the country. In 1948, released time classes held in public school classrooms were declared unconstitutional in a case brought by a parent in Champaign, Illinois. It was deemed a violation of the establishment clause of the First Amendment. This was a severe blow to the growth of the programs around the country, and Weekday Religious Education went into a serious decline, despite a subsequent Supreme Court decision in 1952 declaring released time programs legal that were held off school property and sponsored and paid for by religious groups. Although some denominations have tried to promote Weekday Church Schools in local churches, the movement has remained primarily interdenominational, except for Roman Catholic programs sponsored by the Confraternity of Christian Doctrine. Weekday Religious Education was a logical "alternative" to the Sunday school, but it never seemed to catch on. A new program was inaugurated through the Division of Christian Education of the National Council of Churches with an emphasis on relating Christian Faith to Public School Learnings and giving it a new name, "Through the Week Christian Education." Some churches have tried after-school programs (the Jewish groups have been more successful with these), other churches have tried calling programs "Sunday School on Wednesday, or Thursday" but this alternative to the Sunday school has not yet been fully explored or developed. Perhaps its time is yet to come.

The truth is that the Sunday Church School remains at the center of the average Protestant educational thrust. At a conference titled "Confrontation: Sunday School" held a few years ago, one of the leaders remarked, "The Sunday school will never be more than a small piece of a comprehensive educational program." This may be wishful thinking, a hope, a dream, or a sense of direction, but certainly not a reality. In most Protestant churches, the Sunday Church School still represents the primary focus for the religious education program. One large denomination calls the Sunday school "The Nuclear School," which implies that it is a central part of comprehensive church school plan, but certainly not a "small piece."

From the beginning of the Sunday school movement, in addition to the zeal for spreading the Gospel, there have been certain ingredients that have remained central and crucial to carrying on the work: the development of resource materials to aid the teaching/learning processes; leadership training or development; and providing administrative guidance and help.

In *The Big Little School,* the development of resources is described in vivid fashion, with the early stories, teacher aids, songs—used in Great Britain and imported to the burgeoning Sunday School Movement in the United States and North America—and later the development of indigenous resources for use in the Sunday schools on this side of the Atlantic. Up to the present day, the denominational publishing houses as well as the commercial publishers together produce a gigantic amount of resources for the educational programs of the churches. And let it be said that the giant share are targeted for use in the Sunday Church School setting. At the same time, however, it must be acknowledged that a significantly large number of resources are being made available for new types of programs and settings: intergenerational settings and family clusters, ministries to singles, to older persons, to middle-life crises, learning centers, mobile classrooms, open classrooms, non-traditional settings, et cetera.

For over one hundred years a major study resource for use in the Sunday schools has been the International or Uniform Lesson Series approved by the National Sunday School Convention in Indianapolis in 1872. This was a significant event. The authors of *The Big Little School* report that "some doubtless thought it a decision for eternity." Well, it almost seems to be true. As one who has worked closely with the Committee on the Uniform Series, let it be reported that the series is alive and well. Adult Bible Study based on the Uniform Lesson Outlines still represents the major Bible study resource in use throughout the country. At least forty denominations use the Uniform Outlines as a basis for their basic Bible study curriculum; thirty denominations participate in the committee processes that develop the outlines, six of these are major black denominations, evangelical groups participate in the processes as well. While most of the mainline denominations no longer use the outlines for their childrens' Bible study resources, and some are in the process of developing a new Bible Series for children, the Uniform Outlines for children are still used by most of the black denominations.

Over eight million teacher and student quarterlies are printed yearly based on the Uniform Lesson Outlines, as well as over four million additional supportive materials such as Commentaries, Lesson Digests, Spanish and Braille editions for youth and adults, Calendars, Lesson Cards, Leaflets, etc., etc. As a result of a major consultation on the Uniform Series in 1974, a new and revised Handbook has been published which guides the work of the Committee. Many modifications and changes have occurred throughout the years. The Cycle is now six years instead of seven, and the new Cycle for 1986 to 1992 will be approved after denominational review in 1980. While more that a hundred years is not an eternity, the Uniform Lesson Series is widely used throughout the United States by churches with widely differing backgrounds, evangelicals, liberals, whites, blacks, hispanics.

Joint Educational Development, a partnership of denominations that develop resources and programs together, has a Curriculum Series called "Christian Education: Shared Approaches." Approach number one, Knowing the Word, is a cooperative curriculum based on the Uniform Lesson Outlines. According to official sources it is the most widely used of the four approaches at the adult level. The other three are: Interpreting the Word, Living the Word, and Doing the Word.

There is still tension in curriculum circles between "home grown" curriculum and resources developed and handed down from above. Perhaps one of the staying powers of the Uniform Series is that denominations do use their own writers, are able to give the materials the particular denominational theological and educational positions as well as highlighting special emphases. And then the series has going for it the centrality of Bible study to the faith.

Another crucial element in an effective church school enterprise is training or development of the volunteer. The importance of this was seen very early in the movement when Bishop John Vincent started the "Sunday School Teachers Institutes" in the early 1860s. Leader development has continued to be a concern of the Sunday school movement, and represented a major program in the International Council of Religious Education through the Standard Leadership Curriculum. Scarcely a community in the country was without an accredited Leadership School. Schools were accredited on the basis of teacher qualifications and course descriptions. Certificates of achievement were awarded to students who completed a required number of courses in method and content. An enormous library of leadership text books were developed cooperatively for use in these schools. With the emergence of new denominational curriculum during and following the 1950s, the desire to train leaders in relation to the use of specific denominational curriculum was very strong, and gradually the Standard Leadership Curriculum was phased out.

Christian education has undergone its ups and downs. For a variety of reasons many judicatory positions in Christian education were abolished, as were departments of Christian education in seminaries, and departments of Christian education in Councils of churches. Christian education as such appeared to be in decline. But the church schools have continued. As long as local churches continue to have Sunday schools, Vacation Church Schools, Weekday Religious Education programs, camps and conferences, the need for training local volunteer leaders will continue.

Denominations have sought to meet the needs of leadership development in Christian education through many programs and channels, some through judicatory personnel and others through cooperative arrangements with other denominations. But a new breed has emerged, the independent Christian education consultant, or team of consultants, or the nonprofit incorporated agencies, a prime example being the National Teacher Education Project in Scottsdale, Arizona. As long as we rely on volunteers for the major teacher/leader roles in the local congregations, leader development programs will be necessary as well as in demand.

Skills in planning and administrating the programs in the local churches are the other essential elements, going hand in hand with leader development. There is evidence that denominations are being more sensitive and alert than ever to what the local "grass roots" or "street level" folk are saying and requesting. One senses a greater responsiveness on the part of professionals in Christian education at all levels to the needs and concerns of the local practioners, and a spirit of co-ministry is apparent. Francis Keppel, the former commissioner of education for the United States, once said, "Education is too important to be left to the educators." And we can echo that by saying, "Religious education is too important to be left to the professional religious educators." The lay person is at the center, and is often deeply concerned, capable, and seeking to be involved at all levels of decision making and program development.

There is hope for "new life in the Sunday Schools" in the 1980s. Seminaries that previously abandoned Christian Education or incorporated it as a subdivision of another department are taking a second look, and reevaluating the place of educational ministry in the training of clergy. Councils of Churches or local and regional ecumenical agencies are forming new committees or task forces to take a fresh look at their responsibilities for cooperative educational programs and activities.

The largest Protestant denomination in the United States has an entire department devoted to the advancement of Sunday school work with 157 employees. Another large denomination has been engaged in a four year program, "Decision Point: Church School," in order to (1) nurture and deepen the commitment of persons to Christ and the church through Christian growth and understanding by participation in the church school; (2) approve the quality of teaching and learning in every church; (3) to increase the number of persons who attend and are enrolled in the church schools. The four phases are: A Heritage to Celebrate; A Community That Cares; A Community That Learns; and Into the Next 100 years. That's long range planning!

Another major denomination adopted a resolution at a recent national synod meeting: "Reclaiming Christian Education as a Major Concern in the Life of the Church." Another denomination seeking guidance from the judicatories to determine interest at the local level discovered that religious education headed the list with 67 percent positive responses. These are only samples of the wide interest in all of the denominations at the present time in working for a more effective educational ministry. The 1980s represent an opportunity and challenge sparked by the bicentennial of the founding of the Sunday school movement in Gloucester, England, by Robert Raikes in 1780. The next decade can be a most significant and productive one if used wisely for study, reevaluation for planning for "alternative futures."

It is a helpful sign that churches have not given up on the uniqueness of the Sunday school as an important setting where the faith is explained, shared, lived, with the knowledge and awareness that this faith is not only taught but caught.

And while the history of the Big Little School as related in this book is primarily a history of the Protestant Sunday school movement, it must be recognized that Jews and Roman Catholics have also been using Sunday as a time for religious education opportunities. So together we can celebrate and own the Sunday school as a setting for religious education.

A leading Christian educator in making a plea for a "New-Old School" said:

The Old Sunday school appears to have cared most about creating an environment where people can be religious together, where persons can experience Christian faith and see it witnessed to in the lives of others. The old Sunday school seemed to be aware of the importance of the affections of story telling, of experience, of community building, and role models. . . . Prayer and spiritual life require that we regain our God-given ability to wonder and create, to dream and fantasize, to imagine and envision. We need to be encouraged once again to sing, dance, paint, and act. We need to cultivate our capacities for ecstasy, for appreciating the new, the marvelous, and the mysterious. Sensual awareness and the ability to express ourselves emotionally and non-verbally need encouragement. The affections are as always the heart of the life of faith.

In our search for new forms of religious education, alternatives to the Sunday school, if you will, it is important to hold on to that which we have inherited through our rich past, especially those things which are worth holding on to.

It is a great temptation to want to innovate, change for the sake of change, to follow the pattern of the commercial advertiser by labeling it "A New Product" in order to sell. Ellis Nelson, in a challenge to representatives of two educational departments about to merge in the National Council of Churches, warned us "not to look for what is *new,* but for what is *true.*" Our search in the 1980s for new forms, for alternatives, should be guided strongly by those old forms that have come down to us through history that *are true,* and will remain so throughout eternity.

J. Blaine Fister
Executive Director
Education for Christian Life and Mission
National Council of Churches of
Christ in the U. S. A.

CHAPTER 1

Reaching for "Lost Beginnings"

*The past will have to be examined in regard to its
own future. All history is full of possibilities—
possibilities that have been profited by . . . , seized
and blocked. In this perspective it appears full of
interrupted possibilities, lost beginnings, arrested
onsets upon the future.*[1]

—JÜRGEN MOLTMANN

The road from Maryville to Knoxville runs north for
twenty miles through the virtually flat triangle of bottom-
land formed as the Tennessee and Little Tennessee Rivers
come together. South of Mt. Olive and beyond Fort
Loudon Lake, the Blue Ridge foothills jut up as the larger
stream comes into view. Around some bends and over a
bridge is Knoxville, where dogwood-shaded avenues spiral
out from a business district perched on a cliff. Before the
young Sam Keen was able to follow that route, he knew

another road better—the one from Damascus to Jerusalem. He had never been on that faraway thoroughfare, or in the Judean countryside which he learned earlier than the topography of Tennessee. But he knew that Jesus loved him and would walk with him when he was old enough to get around the state.[2]

Sam Keen the adult—theologian and cogent commentator on America's society and psyche—vividly remembered which geography he knew first and why: The Protestant Sunday school. His experience in Maryville is hardly unique. Millions have memorized the map of the Holy Land before they could get out of home towns. The Sunday school as movement and institution has made an indelible mark on the entire cultural and educational experience of American Protestant generations. But the collective and historical memory of what the Sunday school has done is today generally hazy, clouded by an image of Sunday instruction as a sentimental relic. The dynamics which etched a picture of a Middle-Eastern road in Sam Keen's mind have been and are at work in the United States. For the sake of a nation's understanding of itself, the Sunday school heritage and its lingering influence must be unclouded.

A limited awareness of the guts and marrow of history, while not indigenously American, does prevail throughout the Republic. Presentations of the past are characteristically political, often superficial, and frequently military in outline. The story moves from Indian entanglements to the Revolution, through the Civil War and conflict on the western range, to world wars, then—with a pause for Korea—to Indo-China. The culture-making interaction of ideologies, movements, and nonpolitical institutions seldom comes into the picture except at the edges. The study of popular religion is neglected by the churches as well as by secular scholars. Yet popular religion is reflected in the everyday attitudes and beliefs of vast numbers of people. It may not be the *best* expression of faith or have official ecclesiastical sanction or agree with academic theology—but it is an apt cultural mirror. Popular religion has emotions; its songs and history make for good storytelling.

The best example, indeed the epitome, of popular American Protestantism is the Sunday school, perhaps as old as the nation and part of the stuff of history. Particularly forceful in molding America between the War of 1812 and World War I, the institution is vastly more important than is probably realized by its modern supporters or depreciators or by those non-Protestants who are relatively unaware of its present or earlier forms. In a day when every segment of society is inundated with crises, the need to know how and what shaped the inherited culture is crucial. Any present is linked to the past by obvious or hidden continuities; any future will be affected by the way those continuities are understood and transmitted.

Sunday school history reveals much about America's hidden continuities with the past—hidden partly because the present-day institution is but an echo of what it once was. Even though biblical geography and songs like "Jesus Loves Me" remain essential in conservative and sectarian Protestant classrooms, and routine in those of many middle-class mainline churches, the zeal for them has waned. The fact that the fire is banked, and may or may not again be given fresh fuel, in no way lessens the continuing influence of an energetic history.

Succinctly put, the Sunday school is American Protestantism's training ground. Denominations have established hundreds of colleges and universities, but the Sunday school is the *big* school in matters religious for the Protestant people—originally and especially white people, though it has played a distinctive role in the religious experience and culture of black America. Compared to public education, Sunday school is marginal to American society, yet is an important *little* school in the rearing of the whole nation. The Sunday school is the big little school of the United States.

It is not mere accident that the average citizen is unaware of the institution's far-reaching influence, even if he could trace the road from Damascus to Jerusalem at an early age. For fifty years a hefty and vocal segment of the Protestant forces has preached and predicted its demise, accused the Sunday classes of weakness and excessive gentility, and proposed alternatives for Christian education. The mood of Sunday schools may be an affront to the more rigorous education encouraged by universities. A Sunday school mentality may explain why American Protestant scholarship is so persistently thin. Indeed, the Sunday school class may represent "the most wasted hour of the week." However, the staying power is amazing; no more workable approach to Christian training has been introduced and, for better or worse, Sunday school is an operative mark of most local Protestant churches. On its own turf, the Sunday school has enjoyed more success than failure. In fact, religious reformers of all varieties, social revolutionaries, and civil rights champions would do well to familiarize themselves with Sunday school lore. This is true for two reasons.

First, the movement in earlier decades had a decisive role in shaping institutions and attitudes which are today targets for actual or would-be changemakers. For example, the maintenance of racial separation—which equals racism—was by word and deed nurtured by the Sunday school in periods when strides toward racial interaction could have been most beneficial. And the Protestant work ethic with its almost holy views of competition and prosperity (adopted by immigrant groups as intensely American) was succored in nineteenth-century Sunday schools. Moreover, an anti-Roman Catholic bias was imprinted on many minds by the Sunday training. When blacks strike out against the systemic violence of social structures, or when Catholics challenge laws banning public aid to their schools, both are in part pitted against points of view honed in Sunday schools.

Second, despite all the criticism heaped upon it, the Sunday school emerged as a reform movement and so continued for years. It shared with labor and civil rights movements the hallmark of reform ideology; the hope and confident expectation of a better future. The British Sunday school originally sought to reform both the ignorant poor and a society which ignored the educational needs of the poor. In America the reforming was aimed at illiterates, immigrants, Democrats, alcohol drinkers, assorted "sinners," and whoever else did not happen to share the Sunday school's enthusiasms. In the Anglo-American world the Sunday school prospered as part of Protestantism's "benevolent empire"—out to convert the world by starting with the community at hand.

The story is not infrequently self-righteous and paternalistic; more than a few regrettable and reprehensible incidents can be recorded. Still the Sunday school is a rather good object lesson in how a reform movement succeeds, how success transforms the movement, how the progress of one generation becomes the burden of the next, and how reformers have a way of making new, rigid orthodoxies as though the future should not contain the flexibility they themselves required. The course of the movement's particular thrusts is all the more important because Sunday school became an exportable commodity, sent with missionaries around the globe.

As the major popular vehicle for Protestants, the Sunday school has done some remarkable things. It led toward public, universal education. By reversing its own concept of infants as repositories of original sin, it helped in paving the way for childhood as a time of carefree innocence. Today, it continues as the major educational setting where Protestants are confronted with and urged to question the meaning of destiny and death. Approaches may often have been bluntly otherworldly or illusive, but death has been mentioned—something a public school does not, perhaps cannot, do. And the Sunday school has periodically captured and channeled aspirations of the Protestant majority by offering needed definitions of motives and goals.

Schools on Sundays, of course, have appeared in non-Protestant churches. Catholics sometimes started them in frontier days and more than a few synagogues have Sunday classes for youngsters. But by and large the story is Protestant, for Sunday schools never became the rule in American Catholicism or normative in Judaism. Protestants in the nineteenth century built the public school system to suit themselves, since they often considered non-Protestants aliens at best. Then, with tax-supported general education to their liking, Protestants could settle for weekly religious instruction on Sunday mornings. Catholics found such a scheme unacceptable and developed their own parochial system as a substitute for both public and Sunday schools.

Evoking nostalgia and sweet memory as well as criticism, the Sunday school chronicle stands as an illuminating American epic—too long brushed aside. In the progression from the Sunday school's beginnings to the last third of the twentieth century, a virtual overview of what a nation has thought of itself comes to light.

Notes

1. Jürgen Moltmann, *Theology of Hope* (New York: Harper & Row, 1967), p. 269.
2. Sam Keen, *To a Dancing God* (New York: Harper & Row, 1969), p. 9.

CHAPTER 2

An Idea Whose Time Had Come

The Sunday school: an institution "eminently
adapted to promote the intellectual and moral
culture of the nation, to perpetuate our republican
and religious institutions, and to reconcile
eminent national prosperity with moral purity
and future blessedness."
—From a resolution of the American Sunday
School Union, 1828

The prospect of reconciling "national prosperity with moral purity and future blessedness" is a distinctively American dream, if not obsession. Prosperity and purity—not merely one, but both in full measure—have formed a constant quest from Plymouth Colony to the urban wastes of the twentieth century. Fittingly, Lyman Beecher, a major architect of nineteenth-century evangelical Protestantism, drafted the 1828 resolution in which the

Sunday school took up the dream. Such reconciliation was, in a sense, the holy grail for Beecher and his luminous progeny Henry Ward Beecher and Harriet Beecher Stowe. Today, political and religious rhetoric echoes the prosperity-purity-blessedness triumphalism of the young nation's spiritual mentors. Of course, some modern Americans may wonder whether prosperity and purity can be united. Not Lyman Beecher. For him the coupling was necessary if the United States was to fulfill its true destiny. Future prosperity seemed certain; purity was another matter.

How were "purity" and "future blessedness" to be nurtured? That was *the* question for churchmen of Beecher's stripe in the 1820s, a decade of mingled anxiety and hope. Colonial ways of thinking were outdated and feelings of uneasiness and displacement were developing. State churches, which had earlier symbolized stable morals and manners, were almost completely disestablished, with Connecticut separating the two spheres in 1818 and Massachusetts holding out only until 1833. Beecher was troubled by the loss of an established church as he labored in New England, disturbed that the visible sign of the old order was vanishing before the outline of a new order was yet clear.

Education was poised between old and new. From the past came the conviction, simply stated by Benjamin Rush, the Philadelphia physician who signed the Declaration of Independence: ". . . the only foundation for a useful education in a republic is to be laid in Religion. Without this there can be no virtue, and without virtue there can be no liberty, and liberty is the object and life of all republican government."[1] How could that foundation be laid when, for instance, a Connecticut school visitor in the 1820s found most teachers neglecting prayers? No attempt was made in many schools to offer religious or moral instruction. Catechisms were sometimes recited but scripture was used primarily for reading exercises without note or comment.

Beecher and his fellows, mostly latter-day Puritans, were not inclined to tolerate such casual disregard. Still troubled by the alleged antireligious temper of the French Revolution, they saw a landscape filled with actual and imagined enemies. They were aware of living in a new raw country, bounded on the West by an immense frontier and perched on the edge of an Atlantic basin where fewer allies than challengers put to sea.

Nonetheless, the era was one of fresh breezes, of new possibilities. To use the evangelical explanation, the Spirit was moving along the eastern seacoast and on the frontier. One sign of the Spirit was the Second Great Awakening whose urgency swept eastward from revival camp meetings in Kentucky and Tennessee during the period from 1795 to 1836. The impact of an 1801 spiritual outbreak at Cane Ridge, Kentucky, was enormous: "It was a spasm among the populace, a violent explosion of emotions which for long had been seeking release, an overwhelming portent for the future of the continent."[2] Apprehension was aroused in some eastern quarters by western revivalism, but the East was also stirred by the evangelical conviction that the Holy Spirit was moving God's people to test new possibilities.

New possibilities included new educational institutions, the Protestant theological seminary and the Sunday school. Innovations of the 1810s, both came to prominence in the 1820s, almost simultaneously becoming permanent parts of the pattern and setting—the ecology—of Protestant education. Seminaries emerged as the national institutions for training leaders; Sunday schools were for local people. After the war of 1812, an apparently spontaneous eruption of Sunday schools occurred along the Atlantic seaboard, especially in New England and New York. Hamlets as well as cities were hit by the idea whose time had come.

The idea of Sunday instruction, however, was not created *de novo* in the early 1800s. How old was it? Who was the founder? These were questions in an active guessing game in the heyday of the Sunday school. Genealogical gamesmanship is often a sign of institutional vitality. In this game the British held the edge. The beginnings went back to Robert Raikes in the 1780s. If not Raikes, then Englishmen could point to Hannah Ball, a pious Methodist who gathered a "wild little company" in her home for Sunday instruction as early as 1763. Naturally, Americans claimed the true "first" for the New World, and they thrust forth Methodist founder John Wesley, as English as could be, but reputed to have instructed children on Sunday as early as 1735 while a missionary in Georgia.

Other reported firsts included a mid-eighteenth-century German pietist community in Ephrata, Pennsylvania, and Washington, Connecticut, where in the early 1780s church elders gathered children on the town green to give training in the Bible and Westminster Catechism. Farther south, "in 1787 George Daughaday, a Methodist preacher in Charleston, South Carolina, was drenched with water pumped from a public cistern 'for the crime of conducting a Sunday-school for the benefit of the African children in that vicinity.'"[3] The games go on. Doubtless, many pastors and laymen carried on some sort of instruction on Sunday in many places during the eighteenth century. United States Sunday instruction in 1820 was something old, something new and plenty borrowed—from Great Britain. The American beginnings cannot be understood apart from what was happening across the Atlantic.

Schools for the Poor

The work of Robert Raikes, known as the "father of the Sunday school," began in the 1780s and quickly spread through the English-speaking world. The Gloucester newspaper publisher became an evangelical celebrity. London and Toronto have statues of him; schools—and a few horses—have borne his name; and one enthusiastic neighbor considered Raikes the most important man since the sixteenth-century Protestant Reformers. All this because he decided to educate poor children on the Lord's Day.

Raikes' Gloucester, on the eve of the Industrial Revolution, was a smallish city. The factory system was pre-shadowed in at least one large pin-making shop. Like most cities in Georgian England, Gloucester was a pit of misery, flooded by people from the countryside and exposing the children of the growing urban proletariat to constant abuse, both casual and entrenched. Few, if any, schools existed for these youngsters since most of their "betters" believed education of the poor was economically unsound and socially destructive. The only education was in "charity" or "ragged schools," favorite forms of benevolence among a few courageous and wealthy aristocrats. But most children of the poor worked long hours in factories for six days of the week. Sunday was the day when bands of wandering, unsupervised and often lawless children inflicted damage on the outlying areas. Raikes wrote in his Gloucester *Journal* in 1783, "Farmers and other inhabitants of the towns and villages, complain that they receive more injury

in their property on the Sabbath than all the week besides."

What could have been more natural than for the obser-
vant and benevolent Raikes to start a Sunday charity
school? Some cynics have disputed the purity of his
motives, ascribing his benevolence to annoyance with noisy
children who interrupted his Sunday proofreading of
newscopy. But that is a jaundiced view. More likely reasons
for his interest in Sunday school were inspiration and logic
that have persisted in the movement. Soon after Raikes
succeeded his father as publisher of the *Journal* in 1757 he
committed himself to jail reform and the moral education
of criminals. His attention moved from *crime* to *ignorance*
as a cause of crime and then to *children* and their ignorance. Raikes gradually developed a preoccupation with
reforming the "morals of the lower class." Or, in modern
terms, he wanted to shape preventive measures against
juvenile delinquency.

Such logic has appealed to many adults over the past two
centuries. For example, J. Edgar Hoover, former director
of the Federal Bureau of Investigation, used the same
basic argument in his campaign to keep the Sunday school
strong. Raikes, of course, was no eighteenth-century
crimefighter. He was a gentleman of his day and a person
of genial benevolence. He started his first Sunday charity
school in 1780 or 1781 by hiring a teacher to set up shop in
Gloucester's Sooty Alley. A few years later he wrote of pleasure received in "discovering genius and innate good dis-
positions among this little multitude." Describing the children, he told a correspondent, "Since the establishment of
Sunday schools . . . they are not the ignorant creatures they
were before. They are also become more tractable and
obedient, and less quarrelsome and revengeful."[4]

No one knows exactly how the transformation in morals

which Raikes pointed out was accomplished by Sunday charity schools. It was a complex blend: (1) an unusual adult interest and encouragement, (2) upper-class benevolence with its inevitable measures of condescension, bribery and social coercion, (3) the freedom to learn to read, a remarkable occurrence in the lives of the poor, and (4) a pervasive religious orientation. Raikes was a devout, loyal member of the Church of England. An alumna of Raikes' school later remembered that the founder was "always at church himself" and listened to the children say the Collect for the day "and whoever said it best had a penny."

Conditions in almost all English cities called for something like the Sunday school. When others heard the reports, they picked up the idea. A movement was in the making. William Fox, a London draper and pious Baptist, was particularly enthusiastic. The Sunday school seemed to be the method for realizing his dream of a systematic, universal, scriptural education for the poor. Unable to draw the interest of the established order, Fox made a personal pledge to the goal of teaching all poor Englishmen to read. He was startled "that in a Christian country, a Protestant country too, no provision would be made for the education of poor children, about whom the heathen take so much pain."[5] In 1785, along with several influential men, Fox formed the first organization promoting Sunday schools, "A Society for the establishment and support of Sunday-schools throughout the kingdom of Great Britain." Its purposes are illuminating: "To prevent vice, to encourage industry and virtue, to dispel the ignorance of darkness, to diffuse the light of knowledge, *to bring men cheerfully to submit to their stations.*" [Italics added]

Fox's society raised money to hire teachers, provided Bibles and other needed books and appointed school visitors. It was, in effect, a miniature school system throughout England, although accomplishments of the weekly sessions were less grand than the onslaught against the "ignorance of darkness" mentioned by Fox. The London Society taught reading but not writing. Manual laborers needed to read, according to one of Fox's fellow philanthropists, in order to learn religion and fill up vacant hours but writing was not "necessary or expedient." The benefactors apparently feared that if the poor learned to write, the new-found talent might be used to foment civil strife. Sunday school sponsors agreed that the poor must be kept in their place. Fox himself explained, "There is no intention of raising them [the children] above their common level; for in that case how would our manufactories be carried on, our houses erected and our tables furnished?" The Archbishop of Canterbury, speaking with a society member in 1786, was reported to have noted that "Sunday schools were well adapted to improve the morals of the common people."

Nor were the poor allowed to forget the benevolence of sponsors. Jonas Hanway's 1786 Sunday school manual, first of a long line of such publications, said that "scholars" must be told that a "number of the clergy, nobility, gentry, and others have taken you under their protection. They wish to make you wise." Teachers were supposed to tell pupils, "I am accountable to God and to your benefactors, to do you justice, and to see that none of you be idle and worthless."[6] Soberly conservative, the early Sunday school benefactors retained stiff class lines along with feelings of generosity toward individuals. Their sensitivity to the plight of the poor was unusual for their rank, yet more intense was a desire *not* to be misunderstood by pupils, potential backers or enemies.

The growth of the Sunday charity schools was phenomenal in the 1780s. Enrollment was about 250,000 children by 1787. Raikes' influence as journalist and publicist was helpful in expanding the concept, as was Fox's Society. But the more important cause of the enormous popularity and growth came from the people themselves and the consent of society. For the poor, schools on Sunday represented a start toward a better life. One commoner, asked if he could read, replied, "No sir, I was born in the days in which there were no Sunday schools; but my children can read very prettily."[7] Unlike the older charity institutions, Sunday schools did not incur the hostility or resentment of the poor and they served as an antidote to the church's apathy about religious education. Above all, the Sunday school was an inexpensive way of meeting the educational needs of the common people in England's growing industrial society. Labor was disciplined during the week and religion controlled on Sunday. Nobody's ox was gored, or so it seemed then.

The "Benevolent Empire"

Carrying the Sunday school forward was an evangelical thrust toward a Protestant "benevolent empire." Led by William Wilberforce, the Clapham group set the pace in the Church of England. The Anglican evangelicals were as responsible as the Wesleys and their Methodist societies for the "unmistakable improvement in manners and morals of early nineteeth-century England." Wilberforce's "earnest but slight efforts" around 1790 expanded in twenty-five years into "an immense reform movement, well organized and superbly directed . . . and using agencies and resources of a size, number and power not yet fully recognized."[8]

Only slight overstatement is found in the following description of the British "benevolent empire" of which the Sunday school became one part:

There were societies for putting down gin-mills and Sunday fairs and closing cook-shops on Sundays, for sending Bibles, homilies and Prayer Books everywhere and for keeping country girls at home. There were societies for educating infants, and adults, and juveniles, and orphans, and female orphans, and adult orphans, and nearly everybody else, according to the formularies of the Established Church or not according to them but always according to some religious formularies. There were societies for the deaf and dumb, for the insane, for the blind, for the ruptured, for the scrofulous, for the club-footed, for the penitent syphilitic and for the impenitent syphilitic, for legitimate children and illegitimate children, for chimney sweepers' apprentices and against Tom Paine and Shelley; in aid of juvenile prostitutes and against juvenile mendicants; for distressed respectable widows, for poor pious clergymen in the country, for poor females in the maritime districts, for distressed foreigners, for small debtors, for prisoners, for female émigrées, for the deserving poor, for respectable married women and disreputable unmarried women, for sick people in hospitals and sick people out of hospitals, and for simple ordinary sick strangers. . . . Above all there were societies to suppress.[9]

The Sunday school was just one small expression of this incredible voluntary effort. In 1803, for example, two societies were founded: The Society for Superseding the Necessity of Climbing Boys, and the Sunday School Union of London—the latter soon to eclipse Fox's society as the nerve center for a burgeoning enterprise. Although many of its strongest schools were sponsored by Dissenters (Methodists and others), the movement's destiny, at least for a time, was largely in the hands of Anglican evangelicals.

Women were notable in this company. That was nothing new in Sunday school circles, for Sara Trimmer, a contemporary of Raikes and writer of "exemplary tales" for children, was an early champion of the cause. She was a visitor with the royal family and extolled the virtues of the new undertaking to Queen Charlotte, wife of George III. The greatest woman evangelical was Hannah More, a lieutenant in the Wilberforce group and a literary light of the eighteenth century admired by Samuel Johnson. Along with her sister she organized a string of schools in Somerset in which more than 20,000 children of the lower classes learned the habits of industry and piety.

As the Sunday school was taken under the wing of the Wilberforcian coalition, it was attacked by the nonevangelical party within the Established Church. The Archbishop of Canterbury's benign approval of the 1780s lapsed. Sunday classes were accused of being "nurseries of fanaticism," which plainly translated meant the establishment feared sentiments favorable to the French Revolution, that "virus" of the 1790s which Englishmen wanted confined beyond the Channel. The Bishop of Rochester despaired. "Schools of *atheism* and *disloyalty*," he said, "*abound* in this country; schools in the shape and disguise of charity schools and SUNDAY SCHOOLS, in which the minds of the children of the very lowest orders are enlightened; that is to say, taught to despise religion, and the laws, and all subordination."[10]

The bishop's heady and undeserved charge was exactly the kind Raikes, Fox and their collaborators feared, the reason they had disavowed any intent to alter the class system. The unsavory reputation which the Sunday schools acquired for a time had less to do with the French Revolution, however, than with English ecclesiastical politics. High churchmen were in part sniping at the Methodists and indirectly assaulting the evangelicals within the Established Church who had taken up the Sunday school cause. An attack on Wilberforce was the real purpose. Controversy so thickened that as the nineteeth century replaced the eighteenth, Prime Minister William Pitt had to be dissuaded from asking Parliament to suppress the Sunday school.

Opposition did not faze the English evangelicals. They were sustained by a vision providing energy and a sense of rightness about their cause. Their intent, as historian Robert Kelly has said, was to "bring personal purity and sincerity back into private and public life" not by philosophical arguments about moral laws "but by creating in their hearers a cataclysmic sense of their own personal depravity. Only when men were aghast at their own individual barbarism, and convinced thereby of their inevitable destiny in hell, could they begin properly to realize what Evangelicals described as the sweet gifts opened out to them by the forgiving love and sacrifice of Jesus Christ."[11]

An Anglo-American Community

The pattern in which Sunday schools were taken over by empire-building evangelicals was repeated in America. Benevolent individuals in the New World, however, borrowed the model of Sunday charity schools from Britain before the Wilberforce group took over the leadership. Just seven years after the end of the Revolutionary War— about a decade after Raikes' first school opened— prominent Philadelphians formed the First Day Society. The Pennsylvania organization was almost a carbon copy of the society launched by Fox, though the borrowing had to be done discreetly in the period of anglophobia following the war. Echoing the intentions of Raikes and Fox, the First Day Society set about to instruct "the offsprings of indigent parents" on Sunday, a day which is often "employed to the worst of purposes, the depravity of morals and manners."

Philadelphia's Sunday school society marked the start of

a common school system for the children of that city's poor and its work was an early experiment in American pluralism. Sponsors included Dr. Rush, a Universalist layman as well as physician and Founding Father, Mathew Carey, Roman Catholic layman, and William White, the Protestant Episcopal Bishop of Pennsylvania. Bishop White heard of Sunday schools when he went to London for his consecration and was one of those transporting the idea to America. Imitation of British Sunday school ways continued in the new nation through the 1790s and into the early decades of the nineteenth century. At the same time, the movement increasingly came under the evangelical umbrella which meant that pluralistic coalitions of sponsors were not to prevail in the unfolding history. An Anglo-American community of shared attitudes was developing during that same period between evangelicals facing one another across the North Atlantic. Despite the enormous distance, uncertain mails and fractures created by the parting of 1776, members of this community "visited one another, . . . founded great circles of transatlantic families, and launched into reform movements in church and secular society together."[12] Frequently, the evangelical network coincided with commercial and economic patterns. Philadelphia, New York and Boston were the American cities where Sunday schools first flourished. In these seaports many emerging Sunday school leaders were merchants in touch with the British.

The extent and importance of intercontinental evangelical ties for the American "benevolent empire" in general and the Sunday school in particular are illustrated by the experience of two ladies of the same New York family. The multiple concerns of Isabella Graham and her daughter Joanna Bethune demonstrated creative borrowing from Britain and the beginnings of a bewildering array of benevolent agencies, generally nondenominational and pulsating with evangelical fervor. The Graham-Bethune career also shows the continuation in America of the precedent of women's leadership set by Sarah Trimmer and Hannah More in England.

Mrs. Graham kept in close touch with her friends in Scotland. "The interchange of pious sentiments," as her biographer gently put it, was valued on both sides of the Atlantic. When she received sermons, tracts and reports on revivals from abroad, Mrs. Graham gathered her friends to share the news and to pray for guidance about their responsibilities in America. These interchanges produced such efforts as a society for sending missionaries to Indians and poor settlers on the frontier and the "Society for the Relief of Poor Widows with Small Children," forerunner of the New York Orphan Asylum.

Sunday schools in America got an extra boost after Mrs. Bethune visited Scotland early in the nineteenth century. She discovered the Edinburgh Gratis Sabbath-School Society, and so found a new cause for America. Following much correspondence with friends in England, she brought about the Female Union for the Promotion of Sabbath Schools in New York City in 1816. The constitution was lifted from the Bristol Sunday School Union with "very few alterations." Plagiarism of purpose and structure was frequent.

The women Sunday school advocates of the early years were not avowedly, or perhaps even self-consciously, plugging for their own empowerment or recognition. But they were taking advantage of one of the few places in church life where women's initiative was possible. Mrs. Bethune put the word "female" in the title of her organization deliberately. She was, however, hesitant in unfurling her female union since some unanswered questions lurked around the Sunday school. Should one engage in a covert form of Sabbath-breaking by teaching? Much of the New York clergy was indifferent to the question as well as to the Sunday school movement while laymen were slow to respond to Mrs. Bethune's appeals for support. Mr. Bethune is said to have finally told his wife there was no "use in waiting for the men" and that she should gather ladies of "different denominations"[13] to begin the work themselves. Fairness requires the addition that her husband was instrumental in starting the New York Sunday School Union Society, limited to male benefactors.

The backing of "pious women" was generally helpful when the Sunday school met opposition, as it did occasionally from clergy and laymen. A typical example of resistance occurred in 1817 in Medway, Massachusetts, where women wanted a school. The young minister withheld his nod almost as long as the deacons. Skeptical men commented, "These young folks are taking too much upon themselves"; and with a shrug of sarcasm some said, "These women will be in the pulpit next."[14]

In the Sunday classrooms the women were, indeed, increasingly found, telling the "exemplary tales" of Sarah Trimmer and other British writers whose materials they cheerfully plundered. American evangelicals needed tracts and books for the children of seaport or frontier towns and they produced little independent literature until later in the nineteenth century. It is rather amusing to imagine a boy in western Pennsylvania in 1817 reading such indubitably English fare as "Tom Trifles and Peter Player," a grim story about sloth, but such material was provided. For all the humor and the accompanying embarrassment, the dissimilarities of a frontier lad in America and a London youngster are less important for the history of the Sunday school than the experience and sense of common purpose shared by the transatlantic evangelicals.

A Margin of Difference

Differences in British and American Sunday schools began to emerge in the 1820s. Despite the similarities in evangelical point of view and the American borrowing, departures were inevitable in the New World. The first margin of difference was in constituencies. The early nineteenth-century English Sunday schools remained, for all practical purposes, institutions for children of the poor. Those in America became more inclusive.

In 1889 the Lord Mayor of London recalled that when he was growing up around mid-century many of the lower class received their education in Sunday schools. The one-day charity institution long continued as the creation of benevolence in which all concerned were constantly aware of the social distance between donor and recipient. An 1813 public notice inviting poor parents to send their children to Sunday school and berating them for not doing so earlier began, "It is much to be lamented, that while the Benevolent and Humane are exerting themselves for your Children's Benefit, that you should be so careless of their best Interests." Forty years later the sentiment had not yet disappeared.

The initial American Sunday schools, such as those of the Philadelphia First Day Society, were devoted almost exclusively to instructing the poor in reading and writing. A class-oriented enterprise could not survive long, however, in a nation priding itself on democratic equality. Class differences, of course, existed in the national period following the War of 1812, but explicit focus on class lines among whites was unpopular. (All twenty-two states in

1820 had *caste* rather than *class* systems when it came to black-white relations. The main difference between the eleven free and eleven slave states was in the legal definition of caste.) The poor were uninterested in special schools for themselves. "The feeling that it was intended for *the poor*, kept both the poor and the rich from attending it," a churchman said of a Pittsburgh Sunday school in 1809.[15]

Pragmatic founding fathers of the American Sunday school tried the opposite tack. When Lyman Beecher was an old man looking back, he explained how he and others prevented the Sunday school's ruination when they realized the poor would not go. He went to the best families in town, imploring them to send their children to the Sunday schools to mingle with the poor. The persuasive clergyman won some supporters, dispatched his own brood and the plan worked, giving "an unheard of impetus"[16] to the Sunday school and reforming its role.

Similar rescue operations apparently happened with considerable frequency wherever there were Sunday schools. What had begun as an exercise in charity was converted into a prep school for the whole of evangelical America. Was the reform Beecher described simply a ploy to get the children of the poor into a school on Sunday? That conclusion cannot be totally rejected but something more significant, more rooted in the social fabric, was taking place. The myths and realities of American democracy were concentrating in the Sunday school, which was to become a wellspring for the culture considered most American in the eyes of the rest of the world. In a keen observation, one analyst has said that the Sunday school was being upgraded to the "level of middle class respectability which some Americans had attained and the rest refused to admit that they could not attain. On Saturday night the poor scrubbed up. The next morning they dressed up and presented themselves at Sunday school to prove they were just as good as anybody else. It is a tribute to American society that they were received at face value—but that face had to be clean."[17]

At the same time that men like Lyman Beecher were trying to save the Sunday schools by mixing the clientele, the slow spread of public schools was having the same effect. When public schools opened—and it was a slow process—the Sunday schools were freed of the taint of "charity" and released from pressure to teach reading and writing. Religious instruction alone became the main undertaking.

Not incidentally, the shift in focus and function had important consequences for relations of white and black children in northern Sunday schools. As long as the schools were largely for the children of the poor, mixing the races was no great difficulty. The introduction of an inclusiveness cutting across white class lines made the presence of black children embarrassing and troublesome. Only a few integrated schools existed in the North. Generally speaking, the American Sunday school movement faithfully observed the culture's caste demarcations just as the English evangelicals reflected the class lines there. A recorder at the London Sunday School Union penned the following account of a report made by a visiting American on work in Philadelphia:

Among other schools there was . . . one for the little chimney sweeps who were all in that country children of colour—he did not mean from the nature of their occupation (a laugh) but that they were naturally born so, and the effect of the Sunday schools on this previously-neglected class of children was really astonishing—they had formerly been among the most debased and ignorant classes of persons in the whole city of Philadelphia; but now such an alternation has taken place that the Song of Solomon might be heard from their lips as they passed along to their morning work.[18]

While a widespread and probably unconscious acceptance of caste barriers prevailed in the North, the South was slow to adopt the Sunday school, partly because it was identified, indeed often equated, with black education. After 1831 southern whites had the memory of Nat Turner's revolt to remind them of what literacy and uncontrolled black religion could stir up. The image of Sunday schools as places to educate blacks is probably one reason Baptists in the South were reluctant to enter the movement, and Sunday school work in Mississippi proceeded very slowly.

In sum, the margin of difference between the English and American Sunday schools which could be seen in the 1820s grew wider as the reality and challenge of the West came crashing in upon the New World Protestant consciousness during the third and fourth decades of the nineteenth century. The frontier—the vast reaches of the Mississippi Valley—held the future nexus of power which would finally determine the young nation's destiny.

Men such as Lyman Beecher knew the scepter was passing from East to West. If the religious and republican institutions were not perpetuated beyond the Appalachian Mountains then reconciliation of prosperity and purity would not be continued. Beecher was not unmindful of the coming crisis as he penned those words in 1828 lauding the Sunday school as reconciler of prosperity and purity and sending it forth as promoter of the "intellectual and moral culture of the nation."

Notes

1. Dagobert D. Runes (ed.), *The Selected Writings of Benjamin Rush* (New York: Philosophical Library, 1947), p. 88.
2. Perry Miller, *The Life of the Mind in America* (New York: Harcourt, Brace and World, Inc., 1965), p. 7.
3. Daniel Dorchester, *Christianity in the United States* (New York: Phillipps and Hunt, 1888), p. 426.
4. G. Webster, *Memoir of Robert Raikes* (Nottingham: G. W. Webster, 1873), p. 15.
5. Joseph Ivimey, *Memoir of William Fox, Esq.* (London: printed for George Wightman, 1831), p. 18.
6. Jonas Hanway, "A Comprehensive Sentimental Book for scholars learning in Sunday Schools," included in *A Comprehensive View of Sunday Schools* (London: N. P., 1786), pp. 12, 13.
7. William Jones, *Memoir of the Rev. Rowland Hill* (London: Henry G. Bohn, 1853), p. 413.
8. Ford K. Brown, *Fathers of the Victorians* (Cambridge at the University Press, 1961), p. 4.
9. Ibid., pp.327–28.
10. Cited by Rowland Hill, *An Apology for Sunday Schools* (London: C. Whittingham, 1801), p. vii.
11. Robert Kelley, *The Transatlantic Persuasion* (New York: Alfred A. Knopf, 1969), p. 157.
12. Ibid., p. 112.
13. George W. Bethune, *Memoirs of Mrs. Joanna Bethune* (New York: Harper & Brothers, 1863), p. 120.
14. E. O. Jameson, *Historical Discourse* (Boston: Alfred Mudge and Son, 1877), p. 82.
15. James I. Brownson, *A History of the First Presbyterian Church of Washington, Pa.* (Washington: 1866), p. 6.
16. R. G. Pardee, *The Sabbath-School Index* (Philadelphia: J. C. Garrigues and Co., 1868), p. 19.
17. Charles I. Foster, *An Errand of Mercy* (Chapel Hill: The University of North Carolina Press, 1960), p. 166.
18. Sunday School Union of London *Proceedings,* Annual Meeting, (May 13, 1828).

CHAPTER 3

In Every Destitute Place

An excitement has gone forth.
—A frontiersman, speaking of the Sunday school

To win and hold the United States for evangelical Protestantism, the "benevolent empire" had to move westward. The Sunday school was a major vehicle for the trek. Log cabin pioneers, first on the frontier, had nature's garden, powder and shot, weather and Indian worries—and the Sunday school. Transient as the rough life itself, it often followed the stouthearted who broke for high timber. Field-to-field settlers who came after the pioneers found in the schools a sense of contact with "back home," scarce books and the promise of culture. When businessmen, the third wave of frontiersmen, arrived, they found Sunday schools as established landmarks.

The Sunday school was there so early and fared so well west of the Applachians that most editors of American history texts and popularizers of frontier manners treat it as normal early American scenery. Yet the process of its spread was neither automatic nor easy. The American Sunday School Union, launched in Philadelphia in 1824, was the "benevolent empire" agency vowing to make sure instruction in morals and faith was available when dry goods merchants brought their bolts to hamlets north of Cincinnati.

In 1830 the American Sunday School Union took on a staggering task, one which, though never fully carried out, furnished the challenge needed to forge a movement. Within two years, and "in reliance upon divine aid," the organization resolved to establish "a Sunday school in every destitute place where it is practicable, throughout the Valley of the Mississippi."[1] The call to the "Valley campaign" and the warm approval by the General Assembly of the Presbyterian Church meeting at the same time were acts of bravado. The Mississippi Valley, as they defined it, stretched from Harrisburg, Pennsylvania, to the Rocky Mountains, from Canada to the Gulf of Mexico. It covered more than two-thirds of what was then the land mass of the nation.

This grandiose *two-year* plan was laid by a new, largely volunteer organization with a three-man staff. Some well-to-do laymen backed the thrust but it was still a shoestring operation progressing mainly on the enthusiasm of its volunteers. The campaign itself provided heroes necessary for the movement. Sunday school conventions from 1830 on thrilled to hear reports of missionaries who had valiantly encountered physical hardships, infidels, "Romanists" and scoffers. The romance of the western experience sustained the morale of volunteers working in more humdrum circumstance. For here was a new cause, a common task embraced by both those who ventured west and the others who stayed home.

The Valley campaign was only one effort to win the West for true patriotism and religion. Five nondenominational societies, each with a part in the shaping of the West, were developed between 1815 and 1826 with a strong core of Congregationalists and Presbyterians in alliance with occasional Methodists, Episcopalians and Baptists. The American Sunday School Union was one. Another, founded in Boston in 1815 to subsidize the training of future ministers, was the American Education Society, which shaped the traditional pattern of theological education; still another, the American Home Missionary Society, was set up in New York in 1826 to assist poor congregations in paying pastors and to send ministers to new western settlements. In 1816 the American Bible Society was established in New York to distribute the Testaments, millions of which went to the frontier before 1861; and in the same city nine years later appeared the American Tract Society which issued some 200 million books and tracts prior to the Civil War.

All five societies enjoyed certain common characteristics including a "union principle," earnest founders who sensed impending crisis and the potency of the immediate future, and a determination to discover and hone new strategies. The Valley campaign of the Sunday School Union reflected these marks of the nineteenth-century reform spirit.

"A More Perfect Union"

Evangelical penetration of the Mississippi Valley would have been impossible apart from the "union principle." Leaders of the five societies knew the frontier was too big for any one agency or denomination to win alone; therefore, a cooperative strategy was warp and woof of relations among the organizations themselves. They naturally competed for support while their activities were necessarily complementary. The field was a place of constantly interlacing responsibilities. A Sunday school worker, sent by the Union, distributed Bibles and tracts furnished by other groups. Any Sunday school could become the nucleus for a possible congregation to be organized by the Home Missionary Society which by 1831 had 463 western missionaries promoting the full range of the societies' interests. When Missionary Society personnel started Sunday schools they reported directly to the Union in Philadephia.

The "union principle" was generally a glittering idea during early nineteenth-century decades when the United States—*the* Union—was in the making. No one doubted the reality of religious and political differences, yet unity amid diversity was the paramount hope of the Sunday School Union and others. From within this perspective, the Sunday school strategy was straightforward and unabashedly stated: To ignore, whenever possible, doctrinal and political differences; to be antiseptically *un-denominational* in purpose and practice.

The un-denominational nature was to be questioned later. It seemed essential in the 1830s. Establishment of Sunday schools "in every destitute place" in the sparsely settled Valley was utterly inconceivable, even suicidal, if approached denominationally. Even when the "moral power and religious influence" of all favorably disposed residents were concentrated in a union school," said a Union report, that combined power was "but feebly felt upon the heterogeneous character, and unsettled habits of the surrounding population." The evangelicals were advised to leave their "distinctive peculiarities out of sight, and out of mind"[2] for the sake of teaching the cardinal truths of Christianity. In the pre-ecumenical nineteenth century, necessity and prudence—"out of sight" and "out of mind"—were the most advanced ecumenical ways of working. Caution, and perhaps expediency, was quite clear in instruction given to Sunday school missionaries and in the way libraries were promoted.

The agents assigned to the West in 1832 were charged to be "particularly careful to avoid all controversy or disputes with any who differ from yourself in religious opinions. By all means avoid every thing like sectarianism, or remarks that would in their tendency, wound the feelings of any Christian . . . *On the delicate question of slavery, abstain from all remarks; much injury may result from an indiscreet observation.*" The overriding goal was "to bring every child and youth . . . under the influence of the gospel.[3] Consequently, a tactic of silence and inoffensiveness on social and political questions was judged imperative. Slavery was taboo because it was the most bitter public issue and the most likely to rend a society or school. The Sunday school movement and evangelical Protestantism in general would long be delicate about slavery; delicate, too, after slavery was replaced by organized discrimination. For the most part, Sunday schools were late in discovering a gospel reason for racial equality.

The nonpartisan temper was maintained in the Union's program for gathering and promoting Sunday school libraries. A committee of laymen representing the major denominations made the selections, and any one member could block a publication that violated his denominational sensibilities. This sort of veto politics was necessary if the Sunday School Union was to maintain diplomatic relations with the warring tribes of American Protestants. Juvenile books, for example, were "fitted to children and youth of all classes and characters; they have nothing in them offensive to denominational, sectional, or political preferences, or prejudices."[4]

This strenuous effort to be inoffensive was both praised and criticized. Robert Baird, the great nineteenth-century American church historian, approved the Sunday School Union publications since, lacking anything "repugnant" to doctrines of any evangelical denomination, they were a boon to Christian education in places where churches were too small to act alone. Despite its anxious caution, however, the Union aroused the apprehensions of other churchmen and sometimes met reprisals. Notably unimpressed were those who believed the Valley campaign was part of a covert Presbyterian plot to capture the allegiance of the younger generation. Various non-Presbyterians got the impression that crucial leadership of the Union always turned out to be Presbyterian. Some such suspicion must have crossed the minds of those forming the Methodist Sunday-School Union in 1827. The General Protestant Episcopal Sunday School Union, established in 1826, was another countermove against the ambitious reach of the "un-denominational" agency. Episcopal Bishop William Meade praised the "noble" Sunday School Union but regretted that its material failed to put forth the distinctive traits of the "different denominations connected with the Gospel."[5]

No matter how inoffensive the "union principle" was made, the denomination-oriented churchmen would not be deflected from the chance to shape educational institutions, influence loyalties of the young, increase profits of big business religious publishing, and gain new congregations in the West. But in the 1830s and 1840s American-style denominations were relatively new inventions of Protestant life just coming into their own. Denominational Sunday school unions, which later evolved into boards of Christian education, had not yet gained power in the 1830s. The initiative then rested with the small group directing the American Sunday School Union. Its compelling vision of the future demanded that the West be won lest it be conquered by barbarism. Reverberations of the crusade were long felt in mainstream American culture, Protestant and non-Protestant, where the Sunday school deposited its particular version of the dream of prosperity and purity.

The Threat of Barbarism

The Valley campaign stirred up considerable attention along the Atlantic seaboard in 1830 and 1831. Mass meetings, such as one in Philadelphia which raised over $5,000, were not uncommon. The most interesting gathering spurred by the Sunday school resolution was a joint session of the United States Congress on February 16, 1831. President Andrew Jackson, who was sick, sent regrets, but a host of congressmen and senators assembled to discuss Sunday schools and the West. On the motion of Francis Scott Key, author of the future national anthem, Senator Felix Grundy of Tennessee presided. The senator was a vice president of the Sunday School Union, but his wife holds an even greater distinction in the early history of the movement. In 1820 Mrs. Grundy founded the first Sunday school in Nashville, today the undisputed Sunday school capital of the world, with five or six firms turning out enough religious study material to compete with country music as a leading industry.

Members of Congress heard the "every destitute place" resolution and most subsequent comments were favorable, though a few grumbled. Ohio Congressman Elisha Whittlesey hoped the Union resolution did not imply that the people in the Valley were "more subject to depravity, or more debased in morals" than fellow citizens in the East. His touchiness was appropriate in light of the low opinion

of westerners reflected in numerous bald and conde-
scending arguments for the campaign advanced in the
East. In the famous *Plea for the West,* written in 1835,
Lyman Beecher was slightly more sophisticated than some
promoters. He contended that the question of whether
republican institutions could be reconciled with universal
suffrage would be answered in the West and westerners
needed help in meeting the challenge, particularly in
achieving education of the heart and mind and in per-
petuating law and virtue. Beecher was specific about his
fears. He said the "danger from uneducated minds is aug-
menting daily by the rapid influx of foreign emigrants,
the greater part unacquainted with our institutions, unac-
customed to self-government, inaccessible to education,
and easily accessible to prepossession, and inveterate credulity, and intrigue, and easily embodied and wielded by
sinister design."

"Inveterate credulity," "intrigue," and "sinister design"—
why these words of darkness and malevolence? Sunday
school organizers were willing to speak in such a scarifying
vein partly because such talk raised money in the East.
But the phrases also disclosed a genuine foreboding over
the "barbarism," a double-edged threat to those Sunday
school men who were terrified of Catholics and sometimes
scandalized by Democrats.

Managers of the national benevolent societies feared
that Catholics might come to dominate the Mississippi Valley and might eventually "either control the entire country
through the polls or form an alliance with the ungodly and
thus make good government impossible."[6] In its 1835 annual report the Sunday School Union complained bitterly
about the flood of Catholics moving West. "Catholic
Europe is disgorging her priests, nuns, and treasures" in a
systematic effort to "control education," said the evangeli-

cals. While such claims were remarkably astute appeals to eastern misconceptions, later "know-nothing" sentiments, and the Anglo-Saxon "Native American" movement, the actual situation was quite different. A flood of Catholic immigrants did arrive after 1830, but most—especially the Irish Americans—stayed in eastern cities. Catholic missionary societies were active on the frontier and Jesuits ever-present; yet Catholic and Protestant numerical strength were nowhere comparable. Protestants had the situation well in hand. For example, the Catholic diocese of Cincinnati, one of the strongest in the West, did not get a sustaining parochial school until 1830 and major educational strides did not come until a quarter-century later.

The inflammatory language and bitter feelings which prevailed between Protestant and Catholic in most places were, ironically, overcome on occasion in joint Sunday school work. In the 1840s a clergyman, writing to the American Home Missionary Society, reported that German immigrants and Roman Catholics had started a common Sunday school in Dubuque, Iowa. Doubtless the exacting frontier life prompted many such temporary alliances although, prudently, few were reported to the Sunday School Union in Philadelphia.

Sunday school hierarchs were more discreet in alluding to the second expression of barbarism. Their reports from the West in the 1830s were filled with vague references to disorder, unconstrained passions and violence. Theodore Frelinghuysen, a New Jersey politican, warned the Union that the West would soon lapse into a "universal degeneracy of manners" unless a "reformation of public sentiment" was aided by responsible religious forces. He was speaking in a code language of a nineteenth-century churchman worried about subversion. (A code phrase today is "law and order" and most people know the targets can be those who dissent as well as those who commit crime.)

What did a serious-minded Protestant in the 1830s mean by "universal degeneracy of manners?"[7] No explanation can ignore the Whig clash with the Democrats.

That Andrew Jackson's rise in the West and the expansion of the "benevolent empire" agencies coincided was no accident. The election of the general from Tennessee and his raucous Presidential reception on the night of inauguration made "good men" and aristocrats worry. A quick response was to press the evangelical cause in the West; the Sunday School Union's Valley campaign came little more than a year after President Jackson's first days in Washington.

Most of the Sunday school leaders were of either Whig or conservative persuasion. Characteristic of the type was Frelinghuysen, presiding officer and chief spokesman for the first national convention of Sunday school workers in 1832 and a long-time vice president of the Union. He was an eminent Whig, a U. S. senator (1829–1835) and, as Whig Vice Presidential candidate in 1844, undertook "to join his Christian talents with the political ability of Henry Clay in the hope of gaining a victory for conservatism."[8] Most of all, Frelinghuysen was a confirmed opponent of Jackson, warning "good citizens" against the Democrats and the danger of being too proud of country and liberties. The senator told the 1835 Sunday School Union meeting that pride and an independent spirit were threatening the rule of law. "Resistance," "liberty," "independence," "rights of man" were, in his estimation, "mere watchwords for licentiousness and all misrule" when they grew too familiar and were applied without sound principles.

Frelinghuysen had a remedy for such ills. The Sunday school, if allowed to do its slow but substantial work, would, he believed, help create a godly people, industrious, reliable and impervious to enticements of mischievous politicans like Jackson. The benevolent managers' anxiety over Democrats, their dread of disorder and chaos, put them in the same camp as the early Sunday school organizers in England. Theodore Frelinghuysen had more in common with Hannah More than an American Whig would have wanted to admit in 1835.

A fretful concern undergirded the American Sunday School Union's efforts in the West well into the 1840s. Reports about the "growing but unformed, chaotic, tumultuating society" were used to bring new pressure on supporters. If only the frontier youths were properly trained, the promoters said, then perhaps the nation's future might be more secure. In short, older America was taking no chances with young America.

Political anxieties alone, however, could never have sustained the Valley campaign for long. Another motivation, beyond the desire to spread eastern morals and Whig politics, was equally compelling. Less spectacular and probably more lasting in its imprint on the Sunday school was the evangelical belief that the deeper meaning of the West and its challenges lay in God's providence. The move to establish Sunday schools in every community was the first step toward a *new missionary future*. Many of the leaders in the 1820s and 1830s saw the American West and the world as simultaneous mission fields in one vast undertaking. The West was decisive. If the Valley could be won, America would be free to fulfill its destiny as the new "new Israel," God's beachhead in his *final* triumphal invasion of the world. The task was clear: Christianize America so America can christianize the world. As an integral part of the evangelical apparatus for soul saving and nation shaping, the Sunday school movement was no mere gesture that could be abandoned when life turned sour and idealism waned. The struggling institution was, at least to its foremost proponents, an instrument of God's choosing, one means of realizing his plan for the world. The Valley campaign was really the thrust of destiny.

The lure of destiny was shared by many along the frontier, even in some of those places easterners judged "destitute." A young St. Louis fur trader wrote to his mother in Connecticut not long after the 1830 Union resolution. After saying he had no regrets in going West he went on:

> We are fast growing to a giants statue [sic]. The days of our childhood will soon be past. If nothing but the love of country actuate us something must be done to dispel ignorance & drive away vice. So thought the members of the [Presbyterian] General Assembly when they lately met in Philadelphia. They were however inspired by higher motives. The glory of God & the love of souls influences them. When they passed a resolution to establish Sunday Schools in every settlement in this valley, within the short space of two years, a resolution fraught with greater consequences to the Nation than any ever before adopted.
>
> But why am I speaking of these things. *An excitement has gone forth. An excitement that the power of man can neither gainsay or put down. It exists not in the East alone. It has passed the boundry which separates the East from the Western States. It has reached this place.*
>
> . . . Can teachers but be found to take charge of these schools as they are formed, we may soon hope a different state of things. Sabbath Schools are the only means which the great majority of the people of this State have for the education of their children, and unless these schools are established, books given them, and addequite [sic] teachers found to take charge of them, we cannot expect the children will be any better than their Fathers were. Think it then, My Dear Mother no hardship that you are separated thus far from one of your children but rather rejoice that he is permitted to come & be in some humble part in this great work.[9]

The trapper had many Valley colleagues equally excited by the "great work" and its indisputable role in shaping the future of America and the world. They dreamed of a world where needs are encompassed by benevolence and pledged themselves to make it so. More than anything else, the harnessing of destiny to that dream made the Sunday school forces into a movement.

"A Horse Tempts One to Go too Fast"

"It is an age of great associations, rather than great men," said Gardiner Spring, a New York Presbyterian minister, in explaining the secret of early nineteenth-century evangelical success. He was essentially correct, for the associations and benevolent societies were ingenious and innovative, comparable in the scope of their imaginations to a few civil rights groups of the 1960s. The Sunday School Union, for instance, had a remarkable ability to stretch limited funds over a host of ambitious commitments.

But men and women, not board meetings, did the field work. Some Sunday school workers, particularly women, confined their activities to western home communities but many hundreds became itinerant missionaries ranging over the immense frontier. They were a diverse lot. Sunday school agents were often laymen, though some were ordained; a few had degrees while others claimed two or three years of uncertain schooling; college and seminary students labored during vacations; full-time agents were paid—if at all—the fine sum of one dollar a day; they were hardy and resourceful, if they survived. The life was lonely, transient and exhausting.

The missionaries were urged by the Sunday School Union to walk from village to village. Instructions from Philadelphia said "a horse tempts one to go too fast. Besides the missionary is generally welcome, because he can talk as well as eat. His horse is unwelcome, because he eats but cannot talk." Better than beast or buggy were a walking staff and "a good satchel well stored with specimens of library books, and catalogues to show, and miscellaneous books to sell, and tracts and papers to give away."[10] The Union felt that if the work was done thoroughly, an agent needed to go no faster than an invigorating walk would propel him.

Sunday school nomads needed a quickness in using chance encounters and a blunt, direct approach that might startle later generations of liberal Protestants accustomed to a piety of genteel nondirectiveness. John McCullagh, a scrappy Scottish immigrant, was typical of the masters of the trade. He was known as the "Sunday school man of the South" because of his work in the Kentucky hills. One tale about McCullagh tells of his organizing a school on Buckhorn Creek and then meeting a ragged lad Archie, who attended no school and whose baby brother had recently died. The account continued with McCullagh asking:

"Would you like to have a book that tells about a happy world up yonder, where people will never die any more?"

"That I would, sir."

"Well, here it is," said the missionary, pulling out a little Testament. "Sit down, Archie, and let me tell you about it."

They sat down on the log, and the mountain-boy drank in every word Mr. McCullagh told him of Christ, heaven and eternal life. The little fellow's heart was touched, and looking up, he said, "What is your name, Mr. Stranger?"

On being told, he said, "I have heard tell of you before. You is the man what makes Sunday-schools, ain't you? I wish I knowed how to read this little book what tells about Jesus."

"Well, my little man, if you will attend the Sunday-school near the bridge, on Buckhorn Creek, they will teach you."[11]

The more colorful missionaries became celebrities in the East where they told of their work and raised money. They regaled audiences with stories about unfordable brooks, wild animals, drunkards, antimissionary Protestants and debates with infidels and freethinkers. The venerable McCullagh was a favorite in the East and, it should be noted, he had a horse.

The most famous frontier agent was Stephen Paxson, who was, according to a Union official, a "plain, unlettered, irreligious mechanic" before he encountered Sunday school. Paxson was dragooned by his daughter into attending a Sunday morning class in a southern Illinois prairie settlement. He stayed with it, was "converted," picked up the rudiments of literacy, became a neighborhood Sunday school organizer, and was spotted as a man of considerable potential by John Adams. "Father Adams"—very much a Protestant—was headmaster of Andover Academy in Massachusetts, and at the age of seventy started a second career as a Sunday school agent in Illinois. Adams encouraged Paxson to apply for a missionary commission in the 1840s.

In the mid-nineteenth century Paxson and his trusty horse "Raikes," were known in hundreds of hamlets across Illinois and adjoining states. He was, in effect, a "traveling bishop" for the remote sections of the frontier. The missionary took news from one isolated settlement to another, sold his books and materials, distributed tracts and Bibles, taught, counseled, preached, gave Fourth of July orations and organized Sunday schools. In twenty-odd years he established over 1,200 schools, many of which survived and evolved into congregations. Paxson outlined the stages in the process from Sunday school to congregation: "a few papers, books and personal efforts gather in the children; . . . the parents follow; then the prayer-meeting; then the preacher."[12]

Paxson omitted only one step, one not aiming at a con-

gregation but important for communities. That was the
arrival of the "schoolmarm" and the common school. Sunday schools were often seedbeds for both church and public education, sometimes being deliberately designed as
forerunners of more adequate public school systems. The
Indiana Sabbath School Union enunciated precisely such a
plan in 1827. "Let Sabbath Schools be established wherever it is practicable," said the policy. "They will answer the
double purpose of paving the way for common schools,
and of serving as a substitute till they are generally
formed. Parents and children, being sensible to the sweets
and the benefits of learning, will unite in one loud and
determined call for the permanent means of education."[13]
Occasionally, and not surprisingly, Sunday schools were
pressed into service as almost permanent substitutes for
public schools which failed to arrive. Sunday schools were
cheap and boasted of a good record in providing basic
literacy. As late as 1858 the American Union was still selling "hundreds of thousands" of its Spelling-Books across
the nation. Sales were made to public schools but the bulk
went to Sunday schools. One missionary in the South
proudly reported knowing of one hundred persons who
were taught the alphabet on Sundays in a period of eigh-
teen months. Politicians in the West were sometimes tempt-
ed to let the Sunday schools, rather than public schools,
serve the poor and sparsely settled neighborhoods or else
by second-rate schools for immigrants. In Wisconsin, one
Milwaukee delegate to the state constitutional convention
of 1847 suggested that the foreign-born might learn English in the Sunday school since they often felt uncomfort-
able in the common schools. Though the money-saving
gambit was rejected in Wisconsin, it remained a tempting
option for others along the frontier.
Just as the western Sunday schools served multiple pur-

poses, so did the missionaries sent out by the Union and the denominational societies. Often untrained and barely literate, these agents were sometimes the only educational "experts" known to local workers in the new states and territories. They never spent much time in any one place because the managers in the East wanted better statistics—more schools—rather than extensive care of established outposts. But at least they could leave behind "Sunday school libraries" which they were commissioned to sell. As the missionaries went from village to village, with the aid of a horse or a walking staff, they took catalogues of Union materials. The society went into book publishing in its first year, 1824–1825, when it offered alphabet primers, spelling books, hymnals, catechisms to suit nondenominational or denominational settings, Bibles and a wide variety of tracts or stories, most of which were lifted from English publications. For ten cents a copy, Hannah More's "The Shepherd of Salisbury Plain" was available, or for a total of 12½ cents both installments of "The Dairyman's Daughter (an authentic and Interesting Narrative)." The hymn book was $6 per 100, unless it was bound in sheepskin which raised the price to $14. Small reward tickets, in blue or red with a scripture text on each, were $1 per 1,000. "The Sunday School Teacher's Guide," by the Reverend J. A. James, abridged and revised by the Committee on Publications, 90 pages, was 14 cents.

At first the Union's Committee on Publication admitted to being "*dictators to the consciences of thousands of immortal beings.*" Although that phrase was soon dropped from committee reports, members continued to be willing to become "responsible arbiters . . . rather than tamely issue sentiments which, in their consciences, they believe to be false, or inconsistent with the purity of divine truth."[14] In 1830 the committee condemned fiction as "silly stories, the very titles of which disgrace the annals of education." It approved of the "prodigious leap" from *Mother Goose's Melodies* to Taylor's *Hymns for Infant Minds,* a better source of "intellectual and moral improvement."

Agents for the Sunday School Union had nothing less to do than "supply the whole youthful population of a country with rational and profitable books." One indication of substantial success in mid-nineteenth-century decades came in an 1859 *Manual of Public Libraries.* Out of more than 50,000 such libraries in the country, 30,000 were in Sunday schools, 18,000 in other schools and nearly 3,000 in city and town collections. That the Sunday school libraries were considered *public* is significant. In many places, especially villages and rural areas, these were the only sources of books available to any who could read.

The Sunday school movement managed to provide three-fifths of the American libraries by 1859 for at least three reasons. First, the Sunday School Union published inexpensive books. As an enthusiast said in 1831, the Union "gives a child a testament and teaches him to read for 37 cents." In the late 1830s the first "Sunday School and Family Library" was developed. The collection of "100 select volumes from 72 to 252 pages, substantially bound" sold for just $10. True, *The History of Robinson Crusoe* was missing but there was the story of a *Scottish Farmer,* a work on Bedouin Arabs and the tale of an *Affectionate Daughter-in-Law.*

Second, missionaries were under strict instructions not to leave a struggling new Sunday school without first selling it a library. If necessary, $5 could be offered out of funds supplied by eastern backers. The library was the true mark of a *bona fide* Sunday school. Finally, the libraries proved to be popular in many places. If immigrants from Protestant Europe decided to learn to read

English, the Sunday school could furnish the practice texts. To those who came West from the eastern seaboard, the libraries signified learning and culture in an otherwise raw and brutish life far removed from "home." A rare Sunday school agent, such as John Adams, could "bring back recollections of a cultured Eastern home." But he always had to move on; meanwhile, the books remained as a visible and permanent reminder of a receding past.

The Union's editors in Philadelphia knew how to appeal to this nostalgia. Few of their publications were more revealing than *The Daisydingle Sunday-School,* the story of what presumably happened in an Indiana wilderness town in the 1840s. In a crude village one little girl remembers her New England home and happy Sundays there. Her accounts awaken "vague hopes" in the hearts of other children. Arrives then an eastern relative who, finding no church or Sunday school, later sends "quite a nice library, of one hundred volumes . . . and some two or three dozen Testaments and Hymnbooks besides, which were all snugly packed in a box, and sent from Philadelphia by canal, steamboat, railroad, and wagon." "Daisydingle" had a big day when the box arrived, for it was a marvelous sight to see children "rejoice in the prospect of new books to read—story books with red or green backs and gilt letters, and pictures in them besides."[15]

This tale, a compound of sentiment, "sales pitch" and appeal for eastern money, also reflected the situation of many a wilderness area like "Daisydingle." Books were scarce, the Union had few competitors, and the Sunday school missionaries were usually the first visitors to settlements. They left a lasting imprint on the Middle West. Perhaps the most important contributions of these now forgotten educators were the omnipresent Sunday school libraries, whose tattered remains can still be unearthed in church basements.

Other Frontiers, Partly Explored

The Valley campaign was a considerable success despite several setbacks. An economic depression, the Panic of 1837, hit all the national benevolent societies. The Sunday School Union never fully recovered the enormity of its previous momentum but neither did it collapse. Denominational Sunday school societies took up the slack and the movement boomed in the Valley. By the eve of the Civil War the most promising younger leaders were in Illinois, where Stephen Paxson and others had labored so long. This shift of power from East to West, carrying out the predictions of the 1830s, became more evident after the North-South strife was over. The missionaries had done their work. Indeed, the success of the Valley campaign was so absorbing that it deflected serious attention from relative failure on two other frontiers that would be important and troubling in later years. One frontier was urban; the other was black America.

Particularly after 1840 a new situation was developing in eastern cities. The 1856 Sunday School Union report was straightforward in its abhorrence:

The refuse population of Europe, rolling in vast waves upon our shores, as it passes westward, deposits its dregs upon our seaboard. These congregate in our great cities and send forth their children—a wretched progeny, degraded in the deep degradation of their parents—to be the scavengers, physical and moral, of our streets. Mingled with these are also the offcast children of American debauchery, drunkenness, and vice. A class more dangerous to the community . . . can hardly be imagined. And how are they to be reached? The public school and the church are . . . of no avail.

The only answer, the Union concluded, was "mission Sunday schools," latter-day versions of the old charity schools or "ragged schools" and forerunners of the late nineteenth-century "institutional city churches" and settlement houses.

/ Intermittent attempts to establish mission Sunday schools in the cities took place from the 1850s on. But urban "destitute places" never seemed to deserve anything like the support lavished upon the western frontier. The pattern of default was encouraged partly because Sunday school planners, like many Protestants of that time, looked upon the city as the symbol and source of human corruption, a gloomy place compared to the glamorous western mission field. That is not to say cities lacked Sunday schools. In fact, enrollments were high, especially in Boston and New York, with greatest strength in the more settled and prosperous Anglo-Saxon sections. It was an early case of suburbs versus the inner city. The Protestant mindset against urbanization was deeply rooted and the expansive West with its courageous individuals looked ever so much more like a promised land./

The anti-Catholic sentiments of the 1850s also contributed to the slowness in setting up urban Sunday school missions. A distinct flavor of the "Native American" ideology showed through the Sunday School Union's references to "refuse" and "dregs." Frelinghuysen, in one of his last speeches to the Union, spoke bitterly of "the mighty tide of emigration flowing in upon our shores." The old man—the year was 1858—warned that "infidelity and priestcraft have joined hand in hand in unholy alliance to eradicate those ever-living principles of truth upon which the Puritans planted this government." A spirit of distaste and resentment was unwittingly communicated to the potential recipients of mission Sunday school benefits. Predictably, the charity schools were not well received by the poor, as they had not been earlier. Most workers retreated to more familiar baliwicks. After the Civil War the American Sunday School Union concentrated on the rural scene, while mainline denominations stayed close to their migrating middle-class constituencies. The tendency toward default on the urban frontier was characteristic of the movement by the end of the nineteenth century.

The national Sunday school movement's failure on the frontier of black America in pre-Civil War days was probably inevitable. Leaders were profoundly embarrassed by the "problem of the colored people" as they knew it through most of the nineteenth century. The whole black experience was a mystery which the Sunday School Union felt little compulsion to comprehend. Besides, the men launching the Valley campaign did not really expect to find black children in the destitute places of the West. As it turned out, some missionaries did work among black Americans, starting a fair number of "colored" schools and black classes within white schools. These makeshift arrangements were never celebrated or publicized "back East" as were safer, whiter exploits. The risk of giving much attention to a minority was too great.

Black denominations established before 1865 were not, significantly, waiting around for white help in educating their people. In the North the African Methodist Episcopal Church (started in 1787 in Philadelphia) and the African Methodist Episcopal Zion Church (emerging in New York in 1796) went ahead with the formation of schools on Sunday. The development was crucial, for it often provided the only available opportunity for learning. The first black Sunday school in the West was opened by an AME church in Chillicothe, Ohio, in 1829. The same denomination sponsored Sunday education in New England, Pennsylvania, Maryland and Washington, D. C. early in the nineteenth century. In the period between

1830 and 1860, as one black Sunday school missionary put it, "the Sabbath school was made a necessary appendage of the Church." This parallelism of congregation and school followed the typical pattern of all denominational growth. The Sunday school, however, was much more than an appendage in some black communities; it was *the* school, without which there would have been no literacy training at all.

The story of the slave Sunday school in the South is enormously complex and approaches the grotesque. By 1835 all southern states had adopted reactionary legislation making the education of slaves illegal. South Carolina was first in 1740. The more punitive measures against literate slaves came in the early nineteenth century when anxiety over slave insurrections intensified. Actual observance of these laws varied considerably from plantation to plantation within a state during the first three decades of the century. The educational fate of a slave depended on the perspective of his owner. Some masters believed in literate slaves because reading and writing increased the efficiency of the labor force. Other sympathetic whites advocated education as a means of assisting an oppressed class. White missionaries frequently insisted upon teaching for the sake of the slaves' salvation. In all these instances the Sunday school was a natural instrument for realizing goals set by whites. Despite state laws, Sunday instruction flourished intermittently across the South in those years when the Protestant "benevolent empire" was shaping up. Sometimes concerned whites used oral instruction as a subterfuge to evade the intent of the antiliteracy laws.

As cotton became king and the plantation system grew more rigid, many planters experienced apprehension about educated slaves. They feared that the barest training in letters might disturb the peace of the contented field and house hands. Literate slaves who would have been prized property in the eighteenth century were "considered more dangerous than useful" as the nineteenth century progressed. Carter Woodson observed: "Doomed . . . to be half-fed, poorly clad, and driven to death in this cotton kingdom, what need had the slaves for education?"[16]

Slave rebellions of the 1830s added to a growing prejudice against Sunday schools. It was known that Nat Turner's education was "chiefly acquired in the Sunday schools in which 'the text-books for the small children were the ordinary speller and reader, and that for the older Negroes the Bible.'"[17] Those planters who had ignored state prohibitions against teaching slaves were less inclined to do so when they saw Sunday classes as potential breeding grounds for revolution and trouble. In the 1830s oral instruction was strongly discouraged, if not stamped out, in most places. Slave teachers, who had not been unusual, were suppressed.

A few white people responded by arguing for strictly supervised schools run by white missionaries. They reiterated the claim that ignorance, even for slaves, was unproductive. Several denominations took part in a campaign to place white Sunday school workers among blacks. The goal was a *modestly* literate, *always* obedient slave. Charles C. Jones was one of the missionaries who labored among the slaves. In 1842 he wrote one of the first books on the history of black education in America. A well-intentioned man, Jones nevertheless presupposed a caste system and maintained that religious instruction did not produce insubordination. "The Gospel recognizes the condition in which the Negroes are," he wrote, "and inculcates the duties appropriate to it. Ministers are commanded by the Apostle Paul to 'exhort servants to be obedient to their own masters and to please them well in all things. . . .'"[18]

Missionary-run Sunday schools inculcating subservience

were often satisfactory to the plantation whites. A South Carolina slaveowner reportedly said in the pre-Civil War period:

Some years ago my people were a very insubordinate people; it was very hard to get along with them, and the severest measures had to be used; but a few years ago missionary work was begun—the work of the catechism; preachers had to teach as we teach in the Sunday school; their instructions were largely catechetical; and now I go to sleep every night with the sound of the songs and prayers . . . ringing in my ears, and I have now no use for any of the measures that were used before.[19]

A most useful institution, the Sunday school, for some.

Just as the large Sunday school agencies never gave much attention to the black population, they were usually silent on slavery itself and abolition. In this they were quite different from their British counterparts, for Sunday school forces in Great Britain were basically united in an attack on drink, war and slavery, the "trinity of evils" in the estimate of many evangelicals. The American movement focused almost entirely on the "curse of liquor." From its inception, the American Sunday School Union was friendly to the temperance cause and by the 1850s the saloon was commonly considered the "Sunday school of Satan." But the Union had little to say about war, and on slavery it maintained a sterile silence.

Lack of American opposition to slavery was mystifying and disturbing to some of the English brethren. Stephen Tyng, an Episcopal clergyman from Philadelphia, encountered rage when he spoke as the American Sunday School Union representative at the 1842 meeting of the Sunday School Union in London. Some members of his audience could not imagine how anyone could speak for an hour on

American Sunday schools and never once allude to a mission to free the slaves.

As the conflict over slavery grew and the Civil War approached, the Sunday school leaders remained immobilized as a group. However, a fair number of scattered individuals were abolitionists and some Sunday schools supported the antislavery crusade. When a Sunday school superintendent from Oberlin, Ohio, was held two months without trial in Cleveland for work in the "underground railroad," the children of the Oberlin Sabbath School Association—400 of them—conducted in 1859 what may have been the first jail "sit-in." The youngsters went to Cleveland on the invitation of Plymouth Church's Sunday school and filled up the jail, considerably "enlivening" it. Four days after they went home their superintendent was released.

The Oberlin children's stand for the rights of the superintendent was, however, not characteristic of the "glory story" usually reported by the movement's magazines. The jail tale would have constituted a breach of the neutrality on controversial social matters—the stand of most other national Protestant societies. William Lloyd Garrison, kingpin of the Abolitionists, looked upon the "big name" organizations as equally culpable partners in a conspiracy of silence, a policy of complicity instead of neutrality. In 1855 Garrison proposed to the American Antislavery Society that it pass a resolution condemning many groups, including the Sunday School Union, as "being in league and fellowship with the slave-holders of the South, utterly dumb in regard to the slave system, and inflexibly hostile to the antislavery movement." He thought such organizations should be "instantly abandoned by every one claiming to be the friend of liberty and a disciple of Christ."[20]

Garrison's charges were resented but largely ignored. For years the evangelical societies had shied away from those wanting to convert them into antislavery units and would not deviate from a proven policy in the middle of the excruciating tensions of the 1850s. The Sunday School Union could not so much as publicly discuss the coming cataclysm without tearing itself apart. Popular, mass-based voluntary organizations always depend on a consensus that includes workers and donors of utterly different outlooks. To damage that consensus, or even to stretch it, was to risk institutional immolation. Sunday school fathers were not willing to take the risk, choosing rather to play it safe by acting officially as though the "peculiar institution" of slavery should not interfere with the work of their movement. The Sunday school stood impotent before the pervasive powers of the American caste system.

Failure in the cities and inability to face up to slavery's implications were to return later to haunt the institution as it sought to explore the changing meaning of the imperative, enunciated in 1830, "to establish a Sunday school in every destitute place."

Notes

1. American Sunday School Union, *Sixth Annual Report* (1830), p. 3.
2. American Sunday School Union, *Eighth Annual Report* (1832), p. 31.
3. Ibid., p. 32. Italics added.
4. American Sunday School Union, *Eleventh Annual Report* (1835), p. 17.
5. Cited by Dorchester, *op. cit.*, p. 428.
6. Clifford S. Griffin, "Religious Benevolence as Social Control, 1815–1860," *The Mississippi Valley Historical Review* (XLIV, December, 1957), p. 434.

7. Ibid., p. 432.
8. Ibid., p. 430.
9. Letter from files of the St. Louis History Collection, Missouri State Historical Society. Italics added.
10. American Sunday School Union, *Thirteenth Annual Report* (1854), p. 77.
11. Joseph H. McCullagh, *The Sunday School Man of the South* (Philadelphia: American Sunday School Union, 1889), p. 81.
12. B. Paxson Drury, *A Fruitful Life* (Philadelphia: American Sunday School Union, 1882), p. 109.
13. Cited by L. Rudolph, *Hoosier Zion* (New Haven: Yale University Press, 1963), p. 165.
14. The American Sunday School Magazine (I, October, 1824), p. 1. Italics added.
15. *The Daisydingle Sunday-School* (Philadelphia: American Sunday School Union, n.d.), p. 14.
16. Carter Godwin Woodson, *The Education of the Negro Prior to 1861* (New York: G.P. Putnam's Sons, 1915), p. 153–54.
17. Ibid., p. 163.
18. Charles C. Jones, *The Religious Instruction of the Negroes* (Savannah: Thomas Purse, 1842), p. 198.
19. Third International Sunday School Convention, Toronto (1881), p. 171.
20. Anson Phelps Stokes, *Church and State in the United States* (New York: Harper & Brothers, 1950), Vol. II, p. 191.

CHAPTER 4

From Death to Sunbeams: Songs and Stories of the Movement

You ask why I cannot keep my religion to myself? I will tell you, my dear brother. Because I see you are in danger of eternal damnation.[1]

—LEWIS TAPPAN

In their prime, American reform movements sing. Civil rights marchers of the mid-1960s had "We Shall Over-come" to hurl at hecklers and to draw them together. Earlier in the twentieth century the labor forces sang as they struck. One sure sign of labor's demise as a movement appeared when only the older union members could recall the verses of "Solidarity Forever." The Sunday school also sang. Knit together by common memories and even more by vivid expectations of a new future, the movement produced thousands of hymns and songs. The zeal captured in music and no less in stories, is both cause and result of the basic success of the Sunday school.

The best known of all its songs came out of a novel published in 1860. *Say and Seal* was written by two sisters, Anna and Susan Warner, who managed to teach West Point cadets on Sundays as well as to produce best-sellers. Not surprisingly, the plot pivots around the doings of several persons involved in a Sunday school. A sweet girl named Faith Derrick is beloved by John Linden, a devoted Sabbath teacher. Among the scholars is little Johnny Fax. The Warners refused to say whether the names "Faith" and "Fax (facts)" were contrived to juxtapose or just happened.

Central to the story of the triangle is young Johnny's declining health. Despite the ministrations of Miss Derrick and Linden, the boy seems destined to die. When Linden asks what he can do for the lad, Johnny holds up his bony arms to his teacher and says, "Walk—like last night." Linden picks up the feverish child and slowly walks back and forth and for a moment Johnny is quiet. Then he says, "Sing." Still rocking the frail creature in his arms, Linden begins a new song, one Johnny has not heard before. Faith hears every word clearly and distinctly:

Jesus loves me, this I know, / For the Bible tells me so;
Little ones to him belong, / They are weak but he is strong.

Jesus loves me—he who died, / Heaven's gate to open wide;
He will wash away my sin, / Let his little child come in.

Jesus loves me, loves me still, / Though I'm very weak and ill;
From his shining throne on high, / Comes to watch me where I lie.

Jesus loves me—he will stay / Close beside me all the way,
Then his little child will take / Up to heaven for his dear sake.

A few minutes later, before reading some of the boy's favorite verses from the book of Revelation, Linden turns to Faith and says, "We were permitted to show him the way at first, Faith, but he is showing it to us now." Johnny Fax dies.

The new song was set to music in 1861 by William B. Bradbury who added the chorus, "Yes Jesus loves me ... the Bible tells me so." *Say and Seal* and the song, "Jesus Loves Me," came midway in the development of the Sunday school's faith. While the Warner sisters' tale pointed backward, the hymn pointed ahead. Despite the death-tinged lyrics, "Jesus Loves Me" was a sign of the future with its jaunty, cheerful jingle. It set a new style of Sunday school music, one of the songs friendly to people, with melodies that sang themselves and had plenty of "go." The "go" songs became popular in the years from 1860 to 1914 because they reflected an emerging *soft faith,* a more reassuring version of childhood and life's demands.

And so the song anticipated changing concepts. The novel, in contrast, contained many of the conventions found in a long line of Anglo-American religious literature, going back to English evangelical authors in the days of Robert Raikes. Central themes were the constant shadow of death, the importance of the Bible and the child as religious guide. Early nineteenth-century Sunday school books and their eighteenth-century predecessors demanded *hard faith,* a stern and somber vision of childhood and of all life.

Little Adults

If sex is the common preoccupation of Americans in the mid-twentieth century, then death was the obsession of evangelical Protestants in the first half of the nineteenth.

Their stories teemed with dying people; Sunday school books moved toward the predictable, climactic death of a pious hero. Authors lavished such prurient attention on deathbed details that the accounts were almost obscene. Not that deathbed prose was anything new for devout Protestants of England or America. The generation of William Wilberforce and Hannah More was fascinated by the drama of ebbing life. Mrs. More found nothing so interesting, she wrote to a friend, "as the closing scenes of a champion of righteousness."[2] There were many "champions of righteousness" in the literature of the early Sunday school.

A popular title in the Union's first 100-volume library was *A Memorial for Sunday School Boys: being an Authentic Account of the Conversion, Experience, and Happy Deaths of Twelve Boys.* The companion volume for girls had thirteen stories! *A Memorial for Sunday School Boys* was a "reward book," a prize given to those who had memorized huge chunks of Scripture and/or attended regularly. Typical of one of these grisly rewards is the account of the "happy death" of William Quayle, age nine:

William Quayle was born October 21st, 1778. He seemed to have the fear of the Lord from his infancy, which produced in him a holy zeal for the glory of God. This he manifested by frequently reproving sinners, especially his mother; which reproofs, after she was deprived of him caused her much sorrow of heart, on account of her not having paid greater attention to them. He used also often to tell her that God would be angry with her if she did not turn from her evil ways. . . . He would also reprove wicked children . . . playing in the streets.

As soon as he was about three years old, he began to pray every night before he went to bed, which he would never do but on his knees.

He was also very tender hearted; for if his mother chastized any of his little brothers, he would frequently weep over them on account of their folly and suffering. In a word, he spent a life (short as it was) to the glory of God . . . but, if, through any accident or inattention he had done amiss, he would fall down on his knees, and ask pardon immediately.

He pitied the condition of the neighbouring children, because they would not walk in the fear of the Lord. . . . In September, 1787, he was seized with his last sickness, which continued about a fortnight.

When his father used to express his hope that he would recover, he always replied, "I would rather die than stay here." Though a child, he never complained of pain or sickness, but was patient and always resigned to the will of God.

A few minutes before he died, he cried out, "Father! Father! Mother! Mother! O my heaven! My heaven!" He then sung a hymn, and desired his mother to turn him in bed, and instantly fell asleep in the arms of his dear Redeemer, September 24, 1787, in the ninth year of his age.[3]

Happy deaths for saintly children were celebrated in many Sunday school songs. The 1835 hymnbook of the Sunday School Union offered suitable verses for the "Death of a Pious Child," "Death of a Scholar," "Triumph in Death" and "For a Dying Child." Number 275 was "The Fear of Death Removed," which assured the child that "Jesus can make a dying bed / Feel soft as downy pillows are." *Union Melodies* in 1838 added "The Grave." The fourth stanza contained these lines: "Then though the grassy bed, / The cold and gloomy cell, / Should bear my youthful head, / For me it will be well; / Yes, better far than dwelling here, / Away from home another year!" / The stress on dying children in Sunday school song and story seems, at first glance, bloodchilling and perverse. Why this preoccupation with death? / In part it reflected an old Protestant tradition, faithfully observed, and in part the reality of high mortality rates and population-thinning epidemics. Yet there are at least three other sources of equal importance.

1. *Death was not a forbidden topic in the late eighteenth and early nineteenth centuries.* Death was feared but could be dealt with openly in the world of evangelical Protestants because there were far greater terrors. More ominous was the prospect of God's righteous judgment. Sunday school workers disagreed on whether Judgment Day was immediate or temporarily postponed after death. But few disagreed about its inevitability and awe-provoking power. This dread and certainty found expression in the hymns which in the 1835 Sunday School Union book included "Judgment-day," "The Judge" and "The Wicked Child Judged." The last gave unrepentant youngsters a macabre image: "How dreadful, Lord, will be the day / When all the tribes of dead shall rise, / And those who dared to disobey, / Be brought before thy piercing eyes." The "terrors of that day"—a phrase from still another song—were more feared than death. Paradoxically, the terrors allowed a greater freedom in facing death.

2. *Real deathbed scenes were household, if not public, events in contrast to the modern cloistering of death in hospital privacy.* Death was an occasion for a family educational experience when "last words" were viewed as unusually illuminating and the manner of dying was closely observed. People near death were thought close to eternity, and reflections of heaven might be caught in their eyes. And the impact of death, especially that of a child, could inspire others to renew their Christian faith and thus prepare for the "terrors of that day."

3. *The most important single motive for the relentless evangelical emphasis on dying children was that preoccupation with death threw the desperate urgency of life into bold relief.* Obviously a

scare tactic, a strong weapon for pushing people toward "right" action and "true belief," this emphasis was also an affirmation of life, a breakthrough in concepts of the possibilities of childhood. As late as the eighteenth century some religious people acted as though children did not exist. Philippe Ariès has explained, in his brilliant history of family life, why children were often neither heard nor seen. He tells of consolation offered to a seventeenth-century woman after a birth made her "the mother of five 'little brats.'" A neighbor assured her that, "Before they are old enough to bother you, you will have lost half of them, or perhaps all of them." Cruel? Perhaps, by modern standards, but, as Ariès concludes, people in former centuries could not "allow themselves to become too attached to something that was regarded as a probable loss. . . . Nobody thought, as we ordinarily think today, that every child already contained a man's personality. Too many of them died."[4] Indifference can offer protection against crippling loss.

Then along the way in the eighteenth century a shift of monumental importance long in the making, became evident. The first generation of Sunday school champions— like Robert Raikes noticing factory children running rampant on Sundays—took part in the culturally revolutionary discovery of the child. Only the "child" they had in mind was a little adult, utterly different from the popular image held today. Portrayals of children in Sunday school material as late as the 1880s presented miniature adults, like elders in dress, stance, gesture—in everything except size. The similarity did not stop there. An evangelical child was no innocent lamb. His early and deep complicity in the kingdom of Satan and sin was taken for granted; death was not alien and mortality was omnipresent. Life could be compressed into a few years and death a constant companion. The "William Quayles" and "Johnny Faxs," had to live faster and better than the Sunday school equivalents of "Dick and Jane and their dog, Spot" in the mid-twentieth century. In the modern juvenile world death occasionally afflicts animals—a pet, maybe loyal "Spot"—but seldom a human being.

The fast-developing, death-approaching children of the early nineteenth century were capable of considerable accomplishments, particularly in their religious tutelage of adults. Johnny Fax and William Quayle held no monopoly on guidesmanship. A perennial and often varying tale concerns the town drunkard who is wooed back to sobriety and faith by his son, ably aided by the whole Sunday school. Child-sized religious virtuosos could convert servants, parents, older relatives, friends, hardhearted benefactors and strangers. Nobody apparently questioned the credibility of a remarkable little adult who appeared in the first Sunday school book published in America. *Little Henry and His Bearer* was a "reward book" like *A Memorial for Sunday School Boys.* At eight and one-half years of age Henry could read the Bible in two languages, conduct learned arguments about the Christian faith, cite Scripture appropriately in diverse situations and ably assist others toward conversion.

An intense purposefulness and a resolute single-mindedness marked these model children. Not a minute could be wasted on games, play, laughter, the sports of the frivolous and self-indulgent "Tom Trifles." The pleasures of childhood, or pleasures of any kind, were infrequently mentioned at Sunday school. A hymn based on Matthew 16:24 stated it well: "Perish earthly fame and treasure, / Come disaster, scorn and pain; / In thy service pain is pleasure— / With thy favor life is gain." This is not Horatio Alger speaking. The Sunday school heroes were uninterested in being tycoons, or in the comforts of fame, money and prominence. Although they were dutiful and reliable in their chores, they kept their eyes on the one goal worthy of evangelical anxiety and energy—the double accomplishment of repentance of sin and conversion to God's purpose. Conversion was the moment of truth, the decision about the future, *the* choice between perpetual punishment and eternal peace. Heaven and hell were the only future alternatives and the choice was, finally, up to each individual. Other matters such as wealth and privilege faded in comparison with the prospect of a heavenly home. *The Union Spelling Book* of 1838 summed up the sentiment in verse: "It signifies not what our stations have been, / Nor whether we're little or great; / For happiness lies in the temper within, / And not in the outward estate." The pressure for conversion hit both real and "little adults" laboring to measure up to a hard faith.

A Religion of the Heart

Rigorous religion—hard faith—had some virtues suiting it to the frontier's hard times. Indeed, the somber vision of life corresponded to many realities prevailing in East as well as West. It took "little adults" to endure the short, harsh life of childhood, to remain sane through loneliness, disruption and death. The early Sunday school's faith was uncluttered, a simple gospel for plain folks on the move, requiring none of the elaborate doctrinal apparatus of classical Puritan thought and life. A tough-minded confidence about personal destiny was needed and, hopefully, loyal Sunday school members would continue to fight no matter what the odds. Teachers, who were expected to whet the desire for assurance, had their models; one was General Oliver O. Howard, who said to his troops before facing the Confederates: "I am going to lead you in a few days against the enemy; what will be the result of the battles I know not, nor how many of you will come out alive I cannot tell; Oh, if I knew every one of you were saved for God, how differently would I marshal you against the enemy."[5]

Although this sort of untrammeled confidence encouraged fanaticism and absolutism (the corruption of hard faith), it did provide a needed source of energy and an indifference to hazards and uncertainties. The strict outlook, above all, suggested a clear mandate for the Sunday school. Its real business—at least in the estimate of many leaders in the movement—was to be an incubator for the conversion of the young. Nothing else finally mattered. To "save souls," to be a "Teacher in the Sabbath school"[6] was more important, wrote Lewis Tappan to his brother, than being a United States Senator. This concern drove the Sunday school to become a how-to-do-it movement for conversion and made it a natural ally of the revival system pervading nineteenth-century American Protestantism.

Revivalism and the Sunday school had much in common. They tended to read the future in the same stripped-down either/or fashion. They grew simultaneously, shared enemies, and embraced religion as an affair of the heart. A degree of cold logic is detected in the way story writers presented "little adults" capable of persuasive reasoning, but the purpose and impact were emotional. The involvement of the heart, especially in conversion, was essential to evangelicals, decidedly so in the opinion of Charles Finney, the leading revivalist of the mid-nineteenth century. "Finney's basic theorem," historian Perry Miller has noted, "was that everybody can agree upon intellectual propositions. The difference is that some grasp them with the heart, others with only the mind."[7] Actually that "theorem" was "basic" for most evangelical Protestants, whether they were leading a revival or teaching a class on Sunday. The Sunday school movement used the distinction between heart and mind to draw a line between its work and any other institution—for example, the public school. To solve a mathematical equation or to study Shakespeare, according to one leader, was "a mere mental gymnastic." But the Sunday school was unique because its fruits included "practical truth."[8] What could be more practical than choosing the right destiny?/Since the language and logic of Sunday school was "of the heart" the intellect had to take second place/

The mosaic of "hard faith" contained the coming Judgment Day, children as "little adults," man's two alternative futures, the separation of "heart" from "mind," and a conversion-conscious Sunday school mission. All this was part of the conventional wisdom when the Warner sisters wrote *Say and Seal,* launching "Jesus Loves Me." If an explanation of why these things were believed had been requested, Sunday school advocates might well have answered with the song's punchline, "The Bible tells me so." But the Bible was going to tell other stories in post-Civil War America.

The Growth of Innocence

The years following the War brought about subtle changes, barely perceptible at the time, in the Sunday school faith. Familiar symbols and forms were still the vogue. Robert Raikes was the most beloved and the "old-time religion" of the heart seemed good enough for generations to come. However, what the heart required was different in industrial America.

Nowhere is the contrast between the Sunday school in

the early and the late nineteenth century more obvious than in its songs. Indicative of change are lyrics about the Sunday school itself. "The Sabbath School" in the 1838 *Union Melodies* stressed punctuality, obedience and solemnity. An ethos of dour earnestness prevailed, as the two stanzas show:

To Sabbath-school, to Sabbath-school, / We'll haste, we'll haste
  away;
We'll early be at Sabbath-school, / Nor ever stop to play.

At Sabbath-school, at Sabbath-school, / This precious holy day,
We'll careful be at Sabbath-school, / Our lessons well to say.

Fifty years or so later the corresponding song was "The Sunday School Brigade," whose dominant themes were zesty marching, joy, sunshine and "endless day":

Hear the tramp, tramp, tramp of the Sunday-School Brigade,
  Whether rain or shine we are always on parade;
By our Savior led, in the sunshine of His love.
  We are marching on to the land of joy above.

Hear the tramp, tramp, tramp of the Sunday-School Brigade,
  We would win that crown which will never, never fade;
We will trust our King, wheresoever be the way,
  We will follow Him to the realm of endless day.

These verses reflect at least two transitions overtaking the "brigade's" music in the second part of the nineteenth century; dourness gave way to hearty, victory songs bristling with military metaphors, and the terrors of judgment day were mitigated.

   The impact of the Civil War on Sunday school music is undeniable. The military image and the cavalry cadence

resounded in "We are in the Saviour's Army," "I Am a
Little Soldier" and "Hold the Fort" (more popular in the
North than in the South since it was based on an episode
out of General Sherman's march through Georgia.) "Hold
the Fort" was the type of song with "go":

> Ho, my comrades! see the signal waving in the sky!
> Reinforcements now appearing, victory is nigh.
> "Hold the fort, for I am coming," Jesus signals still;
> Wave the answer back to heaven, "By thy grace we will."

The line, "We will follow Him to the realm of endless day"
in the "Sunday School Brigade" is perhaps even more indicative of a shifting emphasis than the march tempo.
Very few of the post-Civil War Sunday school hymns
echoed the grim warnings of Judgment Day. The
mournful "Death of the Pious Child" of the 1830s was
replaced by the upbeat "There's a Great Day Coming."
Two alternative futures were still in style, but what a difference! Evangelicals of an earlier day could never have
spoken of the final disclosure of divine wrath as a "great
day." The nearer the twentieth century came, the more
the Sunday school's songs of judgment sounded like descriptions of a family reunion. Hell was no longer overwhelming in its terrors. The individual's religious worry,
explicated in song, swirled around the fear that God might
somehow overlook him when passing out heaven-bound
tickets. Immortality was the great reward to be claimed
and divine forgetfulness was more threatening than divine
wrath.

"Shall we Gather at the River?" spoke directly to the
possibility of divine carelessness. With words and tune by
the Reverend Robert Lowry, who composed the music for
"I Need Thee Every Hour" and "We're Marching to Zion,"

this hymn first come to national prominence when thousands of youngsters marched through the streets of Brooklyn ("The City of Sunday Schools") in the 1865 Sunday school parade, singing these words:

Shall we gather at the river, / Where bright angel feet have trod;
With its crystal tide forever / Flowing by the throne of God?

Yes, we'll gather at the river, / The beautiful, the beautiful river;
Gather with the saints at the river / That flows by the throne of God.

The reassurance of that "yes" struck home and Lowry's hymn was followed by countless others along the same line. They ranged from the soft, caressing, maternal touch of Fanny Crosby's "Safe in the Arms of Jesus" to the hard-driving aggressiveness of Charlie D. Tillman's "Life's Railway to Heaven," the epitome of the rollicking, almost rolling revival music that swept the Sunday school. And no wonder. Its assurance of heaven and its emphasis on speed, effort and human autonomy meshed nicely with the sense of life in a country undergoing the throes of industrialization. In the first verse came the challenge:

Life is like a mountain railroad, / With an engineer that's brave;
We must make the run successful, / From the cradle to the grave;
Watch the curves, the fills, the tunnels; / Never falter, never quail;
Keep your hand upon the throttle, / And your eye upon the rail.

Then the reward:

As you roll across the trestle, / Spanning Jordan's swelling tide,
You behold the Union Depot / Into which your train will glide;

There you'll meet the Sup'rintendent, / God the Father, God the
    Son,
With the hearty, joyous plaudit, / "Weary pilgrim, welcome
    home."

John Bunyan's pilgrim had come a long way; God was
confined to waiting in a heavenly depot for the arrival of
man, who was the center of activity and power. This was
Calvinism totally unstrung; "salvation" and immortality
had become an achievement rather than a gift. God's sovereignty went, as by subversion, into the shadows.

As the hopeful word about the divine plaudits awaiting
pilgrims at the end was voiced abroad, Sunday school
leaders were also confidently discovering new and better
ways to begin the "run successful." The "little adults" of
stories and songs from pre-Civil War days were increasingly irrelevant. A handful mourned the dwindling popularity of "Little Henry" and his friends, but many Protestants looked upon the older literature as dull books about
unbelievably good children who suffer a premature death.
Off to the basements went the Sunday School Union Library Number 1 with its pious children too good to live. A
modern, *natural* image of childhood was emerging.
The same revolt occurred in the realm of church music.
By the turn of the century the death music of the old-time
Sunday school had acquired a dismal reputation. Such
songs as "The Grave" and "Death of a Pious Child" were
dismissed by the disdainful epithet, "mortuary hymns."
The strongest critic of these songs was the "religious education" movement of the early twentieth century, a group
of reformers sensitive to the promptings of progressive
theories of John Dewey and other liberals. One incipient
reformer condemned mortuary hymns as "unfitted for
childhood" and suggested that such lines as "Hold thou

the cross before my closing eyes, / Shine through the gloom and point me to the skies" were for more mature years. "No healthy, happy child desires to die," he continued. "Sunday school hymnology should exhale a natural, healthy sentiment. It should delight in nature, in God, in Christ, in home and country, and cherish the larger love of mankind. It should be cheerful and joyous like childhood itself, but always chaste, reverent and devotional." He labeled as "false sentiment" the verse blessing Sunday school as that place a "child of grace" would rather stay than spend his hours in play.[9]

These swift and decisive judgments about natural and false sentiment reflected fundamental upheavals taking place at the root of American culture during the presidencies of William McKinley, Theodore Roosevelt and William Howard Taft. It is at the level of what is taken for granted—the obvious, automatic truths—that the most radical changes in societies and nations occur and can be studied. The alert Sunday school leader, from the outset of the twentieth century, could begin to take for granted a different sense of time from that of his predecessor a few generations earlier. One source of this shift in attitude was the improvement in sanitation and ways of controlling disease. A progressive concept of natural childhood presupposed, or even anticipated, a lower rate of mortality. There was time to spare, time to enjoy the pleasures and advantages of a prelude to adulthood. The modern child had breathing space, a freedom from the onslaught of maturity and the distant rumor of death. Work, adulthood, the worries of the world—all these would come soon enough. For a few years at least, the American youngster should enjoy the temporary grace of childhood.

Not all Sunday school workers would have explicitly affirmed the virginal innocence of children. That would have been too abrupt and decisive a break with inherited theological tradition. Yet even the staunchest defender of the doctrine of original sin was affected by the emerging concept of childhood. While orthodox churchmen and the "religious educators" quarreled bitterly in the first decades of the twentieth century, they were united in one crucial respect: both embraced, though in varying degrees, the common ideal of the child as "sunbeam," a notion largely foreign to their evangelical ancestors.

It was an important agreement, for the rise of the "sunbeam" theme in the latter part of the nineteenth century represented a shift in the movement's perception of the child and his relation to nature.

Before the Civil War the Sunday school encouraged scholars to observe the moral character of nature. Nature told children to be industrious, sober and diligent in all things assigned by adults. *An Easy Introduction to the Knowledge of Nature* invited young readers to contemplate the spider, a mentor teaching "little boys and girls . . . both industry and exactness: for their webs are woven with the most perfect regularity." Bees were likewise edifying, since "the young ones learn readily what the old ones show them how to do; and little boys and girls should likewise be desirous of improving from the instructions that are given them."[10]

Different lessons were learned from nature in Sunday schools of the late nineteenth and twentieth centuries. Busy bees and industrious spiders were not entirely forgotten, but the new focus was on nature's beauty, its lovely and playfully delicate ways of expressing life. The carefree, trusting bird told an anxious child that "God is love, God is love, In his tender care, / Safe we rest, safe we rest, He is ev'rywhere."[11] And the flowers said, "God is love, joyfully children sing, / Tell all the glad story of your

King."[12] In the song, "God is Everywhere," children were directed to breezes, shadows, sunlight, trees, flowers, birds and to their own hearts for signs of deity.[13]

In such profusion of beauty, the moral imperative of the Sunday school was a child *to be* rather than *to do*. A life was like a simple sunbeam, a ray of light breaking through dark clouds to brighten the landscape. The Sunday schools became virtual classrooms for sunbeams/ A variety of sunbeam songs have been located. One example, "I Will Be a Sunbeam," suffices:

I will be a sunbeam ev'ry day, / Shining, tho' the skies are drear;
Bringing golden sunshine all the way, / Speaking loving words
    of cheer.
Sunbeams, sunbeams, / Shining for the Saviour far and near;
Bringing golden sunshine all the way, / Speaking loving words
    of cheer.[14]

Sunbeam songs were so commonplace and sometimes so caricatured, that the intended meaning of their creators is hard to discover. Precise origins are also elusive. One of the first appearances of the sunbeam theme in Sunday school literature was in a story, *The Cloud and the Sunbeam,* written by Nellie Grahame and published by the Presbyterians in 1865. The moral was stated: "Bright, smiling faces, and looks of love sometimes brighten even the cares and sorrows of a home, and chase them all away." The narrative centered on a sunbeam who "once came to a saddened home in the shape of a little baby girl [Grace Stanley], with soft, brown eyes, and such a dear, little innocent face that no one could look upon it without loving it."[15] Little Grace became an even purer ray after her conversion. Later in the nineteenth century Nellie Grahame's cautionary note on conversion faded somewhat as *the child as the sunbeam* came into its own as a virtual Sunday school doctrine. Grace Stanley and her successors were persuasive precisely because they were different from mature people, anything but "little adults." The carefree, playful, trusting and dependent sunbeam cast the momentary light of innocence upon an otherwise soiled and troubled world. Sunbeam children may have been created as much to provide momentary escape for Sunday school workers raised under the symbols of hard faith as they were to explain childhood to children.

Bird, flower and sunbeam songs, when taken together, constituted a striking testament of faith in the beneficence of nature. The birds were always happy, breezes gentle and flowers blooming and nodding in the warm sun of a peaceful, serene kingdom. This dreamy, serpentless garden of Eden in the Sunday school outlook is all the more remarkable in light of the religious and cultural anxiety stirred up in late nineteenth-century America by Charles Darwin's *On the Origin of Species* and the debate over the survival of the fittest. If the writers of children's hymns shared Alfred Tennyson's lament about nature "red in tooth and claw," they seldom revealed it. Their prevailing desire was probably to protect children—regardless of how and where the species originated—from the darker side of life and thus preserve innocence as long as possible. The result, whatever the motive, was an incorrigibly sentimental appraisal of childhood and nature.

Sentimentality is the corrupter of any soft faith just as fanaticism and absolutism despoil hard faith. A corrupted sentiment was present, for instance, in the hymn writers' concern for unfortunate children, whether near or far away. Should a local mischief-maker steal a quince or apple, a sunbeam was obliged, as one song put it, to "Tell him to halt! tell him to halt! / Whatever may be his fault."[16]

More often, the unfortunate and needy children were overseas, as was "The Little Hindoo Girl":

> I am a little Hindoo girl, / Of Jesus never heard;
> Oh, pity me, dear Christian child, / Oh, send to me His word.
> Oh, pity me, for I have grief / So great I cannot tell,
> And say if truly there's a heaven, / Where such as I can dwell.

The next verse tells how the "dear Christian child" is speeding the gospel around the globe and will eventually be glad to greet the "little Hindoo girl" before the heavenly throne. Zeal for the ultimate joy of the needy was one response. A sunbeam child could also give practical help to the unfortunate with only a penny, "Not on apples or cakes, or playthings to spend it, / But over the seas to the heathen to send it."[17]

These sentimental songs were attuned to the aspirations and needs of the day in American Protestant culture. Hard faith may have given way to soft faith but religion was still very much an affair of the heart. Moreover, it was the era of the expanding Protestant empire, a time when the mission network circled the globe and people of many lands joined Britishers and Americans in the cry, "Lift up the cross of Jesus, / His banner be unfurled, / Till every tongue confess Him through / The whole wide world."

Sunday schools were being planted on every continent; children in African rain forests, Australian deserts and Alaskan igloos soon had their own versions of "Sunbeams for Jesus" and "Shall We Gather at the River?" None of the songs, however, was more universally adoped than "Jesus Loves Me." Translated into countless languages and dialects—including Hindustani for the "little Hindoo girl"—the poem of the Warner sisters became the alma mater of the Sunday school movement. Doubtless each culture assigned its own meaning to the words. That was fair enough. American Protestants claimed scriptual sanction for their conviction about "Life's Railway to Heaven" and the pure innocence of children. Other nationalities in quite different circumstances could just as legitimately fit their cultural and religious values under the generous canopy of that ever-popular phrase, "this I know, For the Bible tells me so."

Notes

1. Cited by Charles C. Cole, Jr., *The Social Ideas of the Northern Evangelists* (New York: Columbia University Press, 1954), p. 99.
2. Ford K. Brown, op. cit., p. 457.
3. *A Memorial for Sunday School Boys* (Philadelphia: American Sunday School Union, n.d.), pp. 9–11.
4. Philippe Ariès, *Centuries of Childhood* (New York: Vintage Books, 1962), pp. 38, 39.
5. Andrew H. Mills, "A Hundred Years of Sunday School History in Illinois, 1818–1918," *Transactions of the Illinois State Historical Society* (Publication 24 of the Illinois State Historical Library, 1918), p. 103.
6. Cited by Charles C. Cole, Jr., op. cit., p. 99.
7. Perry Miller, op. cit., p. 25.
8. John S. Hart, *The Sunday School Idea* (Philadelphia: J. C. Garrigues & Co., 1874), p. 151.
9. C. W. Wendte, "Sentiment and Song in the Sunday School," *Religious Education* (III), p. 95.
10. *An Easy Introduction to the Knowledge of Nature* (Philadelphia: American Sunday School Union, n.d.), pp. 79, 82.
11. "A Father's Care," *Songs for Little Singers* (Philadelphia: Hall-Mack Company, 1914), p. 43.
12. "What are the Flowers Saying?" *Songs for Little Singers*, p. 22.
13. "God is Everywhere," *Songs for Little Singers*, p. 23.
14. "I Will be a Sunbeam," *Songs for Little Singers*, (ed.) J. Lincoln

Hall and Elsie Duncan Yale (Philadelphia: Hall-Mack Company, 1909), p. 58.

15. Nellie Grahame, *The Cloud and the Sunbeam* (Philadelphia: Presbyterian Board of Publication, 1865), p. 25.

16. "Tell Him to Halt," *Hymnal for Primary Classes* (Philadelphia: American Sunday School Union, 1896), #86.

17. "The Best Use of a Penny," *Hymnal for Primary Classes,* # 126.

CHAPTER 5

A Pinch of Harvard,
A Heap of Tammany Hall

God skimmed the church and poured the cream into the
Sunday school.

—WILLIAM REYNOLDS

The Sunday school movement experienced a "second birth" after the Civil War. Progress from death songs to sunbeams and from children as "little adults" to innocents was involved, but these shifts were partly cultural inevitabilities. The transformation of the Sunday school into *the* worldwide work of evangelical Protestantism was quite deliberately and thoroughly the work of an energetic group of men—the "Illinois Band."

A Northern army camp in 1864 was the setting for the first encounter in the remarkable collaboration which baptized boosterism, almost deified organization and sent "the Army of the Lord" marching toward the twentieth century. Dwight L. Moody, Chicago salesman turned full-time evangelist, and William Reynolds, a Peoria businessman, were doing civilian religious work among the troops. They were, on one occasion, discussing the future. In Reynolds' often told and probably later embellished recollection, Moody proposed that they go into Sunday school activity when the war ended since "teaching the children of this country the way to Christ and then building them up in Christ" was the "greatest work in this world." The evangelist told Reynolds to go to Springfield the next June for a state Sunday school convention. "Let us try to capture that convention and try to make it a power in the State," said Moody.[1] The convention was captured; a power was made in Illinois, and then in most of North America.

Included in the "Illinois Band" were Benjamin F. Jacobs, Baptist layman and produce dealer and later a real estate man in Chicago; John H. Vincent, a young Methodist clergyman; Edward Eggleston, a Sunday school editor and future author of *The Hoosier Schoolmaster;* Reynolds, and a host of lesser lights. Moody went on to bigger things as the leading revivalist of the Anglo-American world, while Jacobs and Vincent became a creative duo, partners in propelling the Sunday school movement for thirty years. These two were unequaled in genius for organization and an ability to attract other potential leaders. They had a flair for educational innovations, some of which have lasted to the present.

Men of a rising generation of evangelical organizers, the "Illinois Band" eventually found ready colleagues in such individuals as John Wanamaker, the enterprising Philadelphia merchant, and H. J. Heinz, of "57 varieties." These men shared striking similarities in background, experience and expectations. Most left home early to work in the cities, and their only college was the proverbial "school of hard knocks." Despite their disregard for the findings of Darwin, Jacobs and many of his cohorts had personally experienced the "survival of the fittest." Cities usually rewarded the aggressive and ambitious recruits, the go-getters who willingly endured long and hard hours; there was no romance in being second best.

A booster spirit was infecting people and cities, particularly in Chicago. One slightly envious Cincinnati resident noted that the Windy City was built on a "wet and miserable" marsh and "made a most beautiful city by pure enthusiasm." The same commentator found a parallel between the great amount of Sunday school work in Chicago and the amount of talk, adding, "But I glory in their talk; if they did not talk so much they would not work so much,"[2] When a city—any city—dubbed itself "the most up-and-coming" in the "greatest state of the Union," Sunday school workers could hardly escape the chamber of commerce outlook, making their cause the "greatest in the world" and themselves the true avant-garde for the whole movement.

The new Sunday school organizers were touched by the urban revivals of the 1850s and accepted, without taint of reservation, the mid-nineteenth-century version of evangelical faith, complete with literal interpretation of the Bible and the second coming of Christ. All except Vincent, who was interested in theological study, were rather indifferent to intellectual issues of the day. Their real interest was elsewhere. They found the problems of organization intriguing and fascinating. Jacobs, Wanamaker and friends took aesthetic delight in transforming an inchoate mass of men and resources into a cleanly developed, purposeful institution. To organize was not just a necessity; it was also the major creative act of life.

Their passion for order must be seen against the post-

Civil War background when the country was caught up in the Gilded Age's accelerating process of change. In one historian's description,

The struggle to organize national life in new patterns, and the search for a viable collective identity ran all through the era's dynamic growth. . . . What economic system could deal equally with a Pacific Coast facing the Orient, an Atlantic Coast competing with Europe, and a Gulf Coast looking toward South America? What did wool producers in Wyoming share with heavily industrialized Pennsylvania or New Jersey? Could a New Yorker understand the full meaning of a California orange that crossed a half-empty continent on a new railroad?[3]

The Sunday school movement, as well as denominations and their education societies, had been split by the war. How would reunion be accomplished? It helped, of course, that none of the prominent northern Sunday school men embraced the abolitionist cause or the "extremism" of John Brown. And after the war they stayed clear of Reconstruction controversies and debates over the rights of freedmen in the South. But there were belligerent memories and the ghosts of dead loved ones from Gettysburg and Chickamauga. Even among genial co-workers in the great Sunday school cause, reunion was difficult.

East-West relations were edgy; the raw boastfulness of the midwestern Sunday school associations did not quite conceal an unspoken resentment against established, complacent ways in the East. Further, considerable differences existed between rural and urban schools. What did workers in sod huts in Kansas have in common with the staffs of mammoth downtown churches in Pittsburgh?

Such questions and uncertainties were unanswered in the late 1860s, yet by the 1890s the evangelical organizers had forged a North American entity out of contradictory impulses and expectations. They were proud of the creation; so proud in fact that one managed, in the course of a single speech, to compare the International Sunday School Convention—built by the "Illinois Band"—to the educational reach of Harvard University and the organizational prowess of Tammany Hall, that erstwhile and infamous Democratic machine in New York City. William Randolph, temporary chairman of the 1896 convention, rated his movement ahead of Harvard but slightly behind that "wonderful organization called Tammany, which I have heard compared with the Sunday-school Association."

Randolph's salute was surely no political endorsement, for almost to a man the northern Sunday school leaders in the late nineteenth century leaned toward the Republican Party. (A Congregational minister quipped in 1871 that he had known "but one Sabbath-school man who was a Democrat."[4]) The tribute was that paid by an evangelical organizer to the true professionals in the organizing enterprise. Randolph went on to explain how Tammany divided New York City into districts, each with reliable contacts, so that any "voter that has to be interviewed" could be reached without fail in twenty-four hours. The Sunday school ideal was similar, said Randolph, and, if perfected, B. F. Jacobs could "put upon the track of a sinner anywhere in this broad land a Christian worker to speak to him of Christ." The emergence of the Tammany model is the real story of the Sunday school convention system.

The Army of the Lord

National Sunday school conventions in the years 1869 to 1914 were somewhat like the quadrennial meetings of the Republicans and Democrats, except there was more lemonade than liquor consumed and not so much overt political conflict. The rise and fall of ambitious men was perhaps more obvious in the party conclaves, while women could vote and take part in Sunday school deliberations. Otherwise the triennial gatherings of the International Sunday School Convention—actually made up of workers from the United States and Canada—were genteel versions of the tribal festivities of politics—spectacles for the pretelevision age, replete with parades, slogans, public rallies, caucuses, musical numbers, group singing and, inevitably, more than enough oratory. The head of each state delegation reported on Sunday school activities, often beginning by praising the beauty of his state, the virtues of its citizens, and the splendor of its Sunday schools. "I have been gratified," said the New Jersey spokesman at the 1890 convention, "at hearing so many of you today tell us that you have the 'best' organization. There are forty-two [the number of states represented] 'best' organizations, and good speakers. I am glad you have them, for we in New Jersey make them and send them out to you."

The booster spirit of these occasions was not just innocent fun. The psychology of "quick growth and high hopes,"[5] the two ingredients in one definition of "boosterism," inspired the swift expansion of the Sunday school movement in the Gilded Age. Quick growth was a fact. After Moody, Jacobs and company captured the Illinois state convention in the 1860s, they discovered the absence of an effective national organization. The American Sunday School Union seemed old and sclerotic, enfeebled by financial troubles and staid programs. The "Illinois Band," along with some easterners, began to push for a nationwide convention system, a series of interconnected annual county and state meetings, with a national event every three years. The makings were all available in embryonic form. Sporadic county and state meetings were held before the Civil War, but the three early national conventions—the 1832 gathering presided over by Theodore Frelinghuysen, an ill-advised, smaller one in 1833 and the 1859 convention in Newark—had done little to give coherence to the system. Evangelical organizers vowed things would be different after the fourth national meeting in 1869, and so they were.

By the time of the "First International Sunday School Convention" in 1875, a scant decade after the "Illinois Band" decided to flex its muscles, the Army of the Lord had reassuring signs that it was getting ready to move. Conventioneers could afford the luxury of the ambitious word "international," for in 1875 a tiny, though official, Canadian delegation attended. The ratio was about twenty-three U.S. delegates for every Canadian! Perhaps a more important symbolic occurrence at the 1875 convention was an unofficial session of the Georgia and South Carolina delegates with their counterparts from Massachusetts "to exchange hearty Christian congratulations." As one Georgian said afterward to the whole convention, "Down in the South, [Massachusetts] has been regarded as a little bigoted and fanatical." He went on to promise, after the laughter died down, that if his old enemies from the Bay State remained true to the Sunday school, then he could say, "God bless Massachusetts!" Given the hard feelings engendered by the Civil War and Reconstruction, this was an event of almost international significance. The evangelical organizers had proved to be adept diplomats.

The "Illinois Band" could be justly proud of their new organization that spanned the North American continent. With scarcely any staff or full-time professional workers, they had developed a voluntary network in most states and Canadian provinces. Soon, they hoped, every township or county would have an annual convention reporting to yearly state assemblies. Thus the triennial national convention would become the nerve center, the heart of a system of communications in which anyone could participate somewhere along the line. The something-for-everybody approach provided the drama and excitement of a mass movement, inspiration and encouragement for teachers, as well as trips for pastors and Sunday school superintendents, and plenty of room for amateurs. Clergy, it should be noted, did not always dominate the proceedings. Here, as nowhere else except the "Y" organizations, Protestant laymen were free from the hobbling constraints of second-class citizenship; they could break loose and exercise decisive leadership in a way seldom welcomed in denominational circles.

Sometimes the Sunday school convention provided a glimpse of a larger church, a more inclusive Christian community that could erase, if only for a few hours or days, the boundaries that walled off evangelical Christians from each other in ordinary parish life. At the 1902 gathering John Potts of Canada summed up twenty-five years of personal experience by describing the Sunday school as "the great 'evangelical alliance' which proves the unity, the spiritual unity, of evangelical Christianity."

Another virtue not often celebrated but nevertheless important was the relatively low cost of running the convention system, which required no sprawling bureaucracies or massive budgets. The convention fathers were fond of recommending the Sunday school as the most economical school in sight: "A minimum of expense, a maximum of benefit," a dictum applying also to the larger system. It was a tidy, thriving operation, an ingenious creation worthy of respect from Tammany Hall strategists.

Yet a big "if" loomed in the future. The convention network could expand as long as a mass of volunteers entertained high hopes. If those thousands of teachers, superintendents and loyal conventiongoers ever wavered in affection, the system was in trouble. The Sunday school movement was, like Chicago, "made . . . by pure enthusiasm" and the organizers were fully aware of this reality, although they could never be too explicit about it. From the 1860s on, a variety of methods was employed to keep the movement growing quickly and filled with high hopes. Most important was an appeal to the Gospel and the spirit of sacrifice and commitment. Then there was pride in home territories, that is, the desire to be a "banner" county or state convention and the stress on the civic function and responsibility of the Sunday school. The "numbers game" was no game to those Victorian Christians. The reassurance of statistical growth was helpful in the care and nurture of volunteers' morale. One of the first staff members of the International Convention was a statistical secretary, the chronicler of growth. His triennial report, an awesomely dull recital of facts, was among the most anticipated highlights of the conventions.

None of these tactics alone, however, would have sustained the momentum needed to keep the convention system operating. It was the foresight of B. F. Jacobs that kept the movement from floundering in the 1880s and 1890s. In the late 1860s the wily generalissimo of the "U.S. Sunday School Army" was preparing another gambit, an idea so simple and fascinating to his co-workers that it became the most talked about innovation in Protestant education since Robert Raikes opened his school for ragged children in Sooty Alley.

A Second Birth

Jacobs' coup was born out of a search for unity and a horror of inefficiency. The "Illinois Band," like many northerners after the Civil War, were enamored of the mystical notion of "Union." It was a natural romance. People were weary of war and had a distaste for any difference that might breed further conflict. Besides, the "Union" had been President Lincoln's guiding star, his principal article of faith, and if the Boys in Blue had fought and died for this cause, then the Sunday school workers could at least attempt to translate its meaning into civic and religious life. But what did "Union" mean? The elusive concept evoked quite different responses. To the practical-minded—who have counterparts in most postwar periods—it suggested the ideal of *uniformity;* uniformity of thought and action, they believed, would create a deeper *unity.*

The imperative of uniformity was doubly alluring to the rising generation of Sunday school leaders, particularly John H. Vincent. As a young pastor in the 1850s, he was appalled by the lack of order and system in the average Sunday school. Teachers could follow their own whims in choosing lesson materials; no common standards governed the recruitment or training of teachers. The result was a state of casual chaos. Methodist Bishop Francis J. McConnell recalled that his memory of Sunday morning in a pre-Vincent childhood was, "'Johnny, read the first verse, Jimmy the second' and so on down to the little fellow who could barely read. 'Have you any questions?' Nobody had. Then tears would come into the teacher's eyes because we didn't seem interested. Then came the collection box, into which we each cast a cent."[6] This condition provoked Vincent into reforms in teaching. If nothing else, the church could take cues from the public school and have faculty meetings and regional normal schools for training teachers.

Vincent started "Sunday-school Teachers' Institutes"

throughout Illinois in the early 1860s. He launched a Chicago-based magazine in 1865 and proposed for the first time a uniform lesson plan that could be followed by teachers in all evangelical denominations. The scheme, entitled, *Two Years with Jesus: A New System of Sunday School Study,* featured all sorts of innovations such as helpful hints for teachers and a weekly "Golden Text" memory selection for pupils. Vincent's idea was a smash hit in Chicago and soon he was called to New York to help the national Methodist Church move in the same direction. His successor as editor of the Chicago *Sunday School Teacher* was Edward Eggleston who quickly developed a series of uniform lessons that attracted a national following.

The Sunday school world was abuzz over Vincent's and Eggleston's work, yet it took Jacobs to make the uniform lesson plan something, in his own inimitable phrase, "for the Sunday-schools of this country not only; but, blessed be God! we hope, for the world!"[7] He pushed it hard at the 1869 convention, but the target date was 1872 when he hoped delegates would adopt this scheme: A Lesson Committee, appointed by the big convention, would draw up a list of scriptural topics for Sunday schools for a seven-year cycle. Each lesson would then be studied by *every person,* from infants to the infirm, in *every Sunday school.*

A simple idea, easily understood, it was not simply or easily sold. Support came from old-time workers in the East but some denominational and independent publishers were fiercely opposed to such meddling. The market for materials offered a growing, often profitable business. Jacobs' plan might subvert denominational loyalty, quell the consumers' hunger for different material and thus affect income. This argument was seldom openly mentioned but its reality was unquestionable. Even Vincent and Eggleston voiced opposition along the way.

ხ ი99ɣ

Evidently knowing something of the special interests brought into committees, Eggleston said that selection of lesson texts "by a committee is fatal to aggressive action."[8]

In the meantime, Jacobs and his lieutenants massed enormous public support and enlisted rank-and-file workers. Delegates felt that they were participating in *the* decision of the century when the matter came up for a vote at the 1872 convention in Indianapolis. Some doubtless thought it a decision for eternity. The official report of that meeting records an intensity of feeling that at times "reached the morally sublime." Jacobs spoke in support of the uniform lessons when the question came up on the agenda. Not a "corporal's guard" was opposed and the victory was greeted by the convention rising to sing the "long-meter doxology."

Jacobs had won; the uniform—or International—lesson system was a fact. Whether the Sunday school had also won was the subject of a controversy that raged for fifty years. No other single action in the movement ever evoked so much praise or condemnation. Supporters defended the plan as though it were a holy cause. Moody spoke of the scheme in reverent tones twenty-four years after the 1872 action. He considered the number of newspapers that printed the weekly lesson "one of the greatest miracles ever wrought in the world" and he prayed that no one "not heaven sent" would be named to the Lesson Committee.[9]

Another observer glancing back after thirty years of experience with the uniform lessons declared that 1872 marked nothing less than the "second birth" of the movement; the point at which "the purposeless, freakish wanderings in the Scripture ceased"[10] and the Sunday schools received, as did Moses, a guiding cloud above the Tabernacle. In short, the way to the promised land was paved by uniform lessons.

Later critics were equally lavish in denunciations. Resentful of "Illinois Band" reforms, the progressive "religious educators" of the early twentieth century seized the uniform plan as a symbol of everything they deplored in the Protestant legacy. Judged by the best modern educational standards, the system was found wanting in most respects. This critique, however, substantially missed the intention of the creators. Originally the plan was a protest against inefficiency; in function and consequence, it soon became a superb organizational device to promote unity and power as well as efficiency. These are results which merit deeper scrutiny.

The World as One Massive Sunday School

Uniform lessons, for a time, gave evangelical Protestantism in the English-speaking world a common language, a Protestant version of the Roman Catholic Latin Mass of pre-Second Vatican Council days. A Sunday school attender from Boise, Idaho, could go into most denominational schools in the United States or in the Anglo-American sphere of influence and almost feel at home. It was true, as a Canadian said, that "whether you enter a Presbyterian, Baptist, Congregational, or a Methodist Sunday school, the same Scripture is read and taught."[11] This sort of uniformity eased the strains of mobility for a restless, constantly moving people. The move could be across town or across the continent; the same familiar, comforting Sunday schools were available. Or if a youngster stayed in one place during childhood, he could alternate between schools and not get much out of step. In a small Kansas town, William Allen White, the future journalist and publisher of the Emporia *Gazette,* went to four Sunday schools "for purely social reasons." At each he could expect the same question, "Now, boys, who knows the Golden Text?"[12] The arrangement was liberating for a gregarious home-town body like Willie White, as well as for a child thousands of miles from home. To be sure, Sunday schools and uniform lessons were also for adults—almost entirely in some modern rural areas with few children—but the overriding incentive throughout the movement has been directed toward the young.

Jacobs' plan heralded ecumenical unity and world brotherhood in an era largely barren of such symbols. American Christians in the closing years of the nineteenth century had few ways of celebrating an essential identity with those of different races, regions, denominations and nations. Sunday school leaders of the 1870s envisioned a new future of boundless possibilities, including complete healing of the breach between North and South. More, they could hope for promotion of "true catholicity of feeling between Christians" which would "strike at the very roots of that narrow, unscriptural, bitter, bigoted sectarianism which has its foundations for the most part in an ignorance of God's Word."[13]

Would not all Christians hear "God's voice speaking to them the same things" if they were studying the same lessons? In retrospect the answer must be, "Not necessarily." The Sunday school vision of true catholicity proved somewhat fanciful, presupposing too much evangelical consensus about the meaning of biblical Christianity. Liturgically oriented churches, such as Episcopal and Lutheran, had considerable difficulty with the plan, if they tried it at all, because the order of lessons did not fit easily into the rhythms of the church year. Evangelical denominations—Baptist, Methodist, Presbyterian—were inclined to oversell their distinctive doctrines in "lesson helps" they sent out to parish schools. Uniform lessons did not hurt denominational publishing, which merely correlated its output with that of the Sunday School Convention cycle. That practice continues even today, for at least one adult series is still the "International Lesson" with themes set by the National Council of Churches and material prepared denominationally.

In another respect, Jacobs' scheme did succeed as a reminder of a larger unity. Uniform lessons fast became the one truly international aspect of the (U.S.-Canada) International Convention. By 1900 more than three million English pupils and teachers were using the lessons; in New Zealand, Australia, Japan, Korea, China and wherever there were British or American missionaries, the same materials were distributed. Uniform lessons were translated into forty languages and dialects for India. Worldwide use reflected the expanding reach of the transatlantic Protestant empire across the globe. The sun may never have set upon the British political empire in the late Victorian era and neither did it on Protestantism's sphere of influence. Protestants might forget the evangelical empire during the week, but they could not easily overlook it on Sunday when they engaged in the International Lesson. Shailer Mathews, a twentieth-century scholar, recalls "something inspiring" in the widespread study of the same Sunday school lesson during his Gilded Age childhood.[14] Some thought the uniform plan a patch of heaven on earth—one school, text and weekly lesson for a durable spiritual empire.

The "Jacobites" wanted to make the Sunday school visible, to put it on the map as a prominent and inescapable feature of the American landscape. One goal was to help the greatest number possible and this could be done only by tapping the secular press. The American Sunday School Union, in the early nineteenth century, was content to publish books, magazines and tracts and to hold occasional public rallies—inadequate methods in a society where newspapers and popular magazines were increasingly the arbiters of public opinion. Generalissimo Jacobs went after the widest publicity for the weekly texts and lesson notes, and the skill of the evangelical organizers in attracting newspaper interest was no small reason why the Sunday school did become visible in the final decades of the nineteenth century. Moody was not unduly exaggerating when he rhapsodized about the miracle of newspaper coverage. The lesson with "Golden Text" was often the big religious news of the week. A spirited competition developed among syndicated columnists who wrote commentaries on Bible passages chosen by Sunday school moguls. For a brief time it seemed as though the International Lesson Committee really was determining the intellectual and religious diet of North American Protestants. Of course, newspaper-reading Catholics and Jews were being exposed to the evangelical point of view. (Perhaps Catholic diocesan weeklies started in part as a reaction to the evangelical domination of religious news in the secular press in the late nineteenth century.)

Members of the Lesson Committee did not pretend to be "dictators of the human conscience," a phrase flamboyantly used by the American Union's Publication Committee. But they were conscious of a new-found prominence which, in turn, brought pressures to yield to the blandishments of special interest groups. Advocates of the missionary cause wanted their fair share of "missionary lessons." Likewise, the Women's Christian Temperance Union (WCTU) insisted on its pound of flesh.

After all, as Frances E. Willard reminded the International Convention of 1890, the ladies with the white ribbons had served the Sunday school well. "We are not an outside force, but part and parcel of yourselves," Miss

Willard declared, noting that out of 466 delegates to the 1889 WCTU convention less than half a dozen remained seated when Sunday school workers were asked to stand. "We rejoice in the international Sunday-school lessons"; she continued, "they are the first great reciprocity treaty among the nations; they are God's blessed John the Baptist of universal peace." Therefore she felt free to make the pitch for payment. "We ask you . . . to give us specific temperance lessons at least four times a year." That was first in a list of requests ending with a pledge to retain no teacher "whose breath reveals familiarity with the wine cup, the beer mug or the demijohn."[15]

Miss Willard's petition was audacious but understandable. The Sunday school had developed into a legitimate target for pressure groups, an unanticipated consequence of visibility. While the evangelical organizers wanted to avoid all controversy, including that sure to result from meeting the WCTU demand, they knew the temperance movement could stir up an even bigger ruckus. But they were comforted by the indirect assurance that Sunday school had "arrived" and the WCTU got its quarterly temperance lessons.

Evangelical Protestant zeal for efficiency reached its pinnacle in Sunday schools using uniform lessons. The degree of efficiency attainable was nowhere better demonstrated than in Philadelphia. One sight to see in 1876 was the city's centennial exposition on American progress. Another was Bethany Sunday School, the largest in North America and, some thought, the best in the world. Bethany itself was a sign of progress, a school attracting, handling and teaching thousands of youngsters. Its creator and major benefactor was John Wanamaker, both a daring merchant and renowned Sunday school superintendent. Wanamaker was dissatisfied with the old religious education and the old mercantile ways. He believed Sunday schools and stores could best serve by being more efficient. For one thing, advertising should be used. His theory was to make an enterprise known, then make it attractive and serviceable. Wanamaker applied similar principles in running his innovative department store and his Sunday school; yet it is incorrect to say the latter was a carbon copy of the merchandise outlet. Sometimes the reverse was true.

The matter of dealing efficiently with throngs of people—the issue Wanamaker confronted and solved at Bethany and at his store—was crucial to the Sunday school movement. The Philadelphia merchant was actually a rarity among local superintendents and the organizers knew the much-heralded "Sunday school Army" was a corps of volunteers with unskilled and often marginal commitment. What they needed was a simple, efficient, sabotage-proof system that could be run by amateurs. Uniform lessons seemed to fill the bill. The system would be a boon to family study, thereby reducing the load on teachers; more substitute teachers would be available since everybody in a community would know the lesson, and teacher training would be simplified.

If the new lesson plan was the answer in dealing with masses, Jacobs and his crowd reasoned, the movement could get on with its fundamental work which was expansion until the life of every single person was touched. Nothing else would suffice. The organizers had a specific vision of the Heavenly City: *the world as one massive Sunday school.* This image of the future reflected a peculiar compound of evangelical passion and American "populism." For the most part, the organizers were evangelical in motivation as well as belief: their business as Christians was to "save souls"! Not all embraced Moody's pessimism about the world as a wrecked vessel, but they accepted his conception of mission as saving as many persons as possible.

The accent was on the mass rather than the single individual and his development.

Sunday school leaders were also faithful to the principle, first enunciated by Lyman Beecher and reflected in the tradition, that the Sunday school belonged to everyone. The populist principle was marshaled in a quarrel with scholarly critics who found the uniform lessons simplistic. Sunday school leaders argued that if they followed the advice of the "intellectuals" their movement would be reduced to a plaything for an elite. A populist-minded speaker at the 1899 International Convention declared his heritage as a "common man" and continued:

I believe that the greatest blessings of the International Lesson System has been that it has been . . . for the use and edification of the common people. A man said to me not long ago, "O, it is not scholarly; you want something scholarly." Well, the average man or woman, boy or girl, is not a bookworm, is not permitted to have a library in his room, to devote himself to theological studies, to scholarly Bible work.

The "Illinois Band" and friends never accepted the verdict of critics who judged uniform lessons inefficient and ineffective as a curriculum base. The scheme was, in short, the monument of a generation, so expressive of a perspective on life that it became the very symbol of the evangelical faith, for its organizers and for those in succeeding generations who shared the same values. Adult classes in northern Alabama and southern Montana still study a temperance lesson once a quarter.

The End of an Era

At the outset of the twentieth century the Sunday school seemed ready for another hundred years of dazzling

growth. Horatio Alger had slipped into the act after all.
Numbers had more than doubled in the thirty years after
the International Convention of 1875. Workers included
the best-known names in American business: John D. Rockefeller was superintendent of a Cleveland Sunday school,
while Mrs. Rockefeller served as head of his primary department and their children were often drafted as supply
teachers; H. J. Heinz, later described by *The Christian Century* as the man "who would rather be remembered as a
Sunday school philanthropist than as the country's most
successful 'pickle man,'"[16] and, of course, John Wanamaker who lived until 1922. When Wanamaker was appointed Postmaster General by President Harrison in
1889, he was willing to let others run the store but not to
give up a weekly trip to Philadelphia to supervise activities
at Bethany.

There were other heartening signs. The first World
Sunday School Convention in 1889 was a triumph for
Anglo-American initiative. Sunday school forces were
chalking up successes in the drive for prohibition. They
claimed to have closed down North Dakota and helped to
undo booze in Kansas and other states. Some sniffed at
Sunday school politics while others saw the movement as a
formidable opponent. In either case, the Sunday school
was deeply involved in controversial matters, thus setting a
precedent for the Social Gospel and later social-action
teachings. Controversies were inevitable if the movement
was to meet the challenges, promises and demands of the
future in a new century. As one worker said in 1902, "God
seems to be offering to America the leadership of the
world. . . . In a peculiar and special sense this International
Convention seems to have been put in trust of the Gospel
and of the world's destiny."[17]

The trust was awesome and so were some of the problems on the horizon, although most partisans had a confident air. Knowledgeable observers were beginning to worry about such problems as finding successors for the "Illinois Band." Jacobs died in 1902. John Vincent was a Methodist bishop, still involved in Sunday school work but also giving considerable energy to that huge cultural enterprise, Chautauqua, which he had helped found as a "National Sabbath-School University." No other leaders of comparable stature had appeared on the scene.

Equally vexing was the criticism heaped upon the uniform lessons. Derisive jokes about "the international game of hop, skip and jump" used by the committee in choosing texts were nothing new. In the 1890s the jeering about "the erratic work of careless shears and paste-pot" was more difficult to ignore. Even among the advocates of prohibition, quarterly temperance lessons were in trouble. "No Lesson Committee," wrote one friendly critic, "can find in the Bible four lessons a year, for five or seven years, that squarely teach total abstinence."[18]

Then, too, the movement had to defend itself against the unwelcome intrusion of modern biblical scholarship, that disconcerting importation of textual and scientific "higher criticism" from the European continent. Within the womblike comfort of a large convention it was reassuring to hear that "Germany would not be in the grip of anti-Biblical criticism today had her children enjoyed equal privileges with ours in the curriculum of the Sabbath school."[19] Or to know that the Sunday school below the Mason-Dixon line was safe because "the religious life of the South has not yielded to some influences, which elsewhere, for a while at least, boded no good to the cause of Christianity. . . . We believe that the old Book can take care of itself."[20]

The Bible emerged as "the old Book," *the* bulwark

against error, something out of the past to be resolutely defended against the evolutionists and theological heretics. While admitting room for biblical scholarship elsewhere, the Lesson Committee reported in 1893 that "we can not have scientific study in the Sunday school. It would require a search with lighted candles to find either higher or lower critics in our ordinary Sunday-school classes." The need, the argument went, was to make the Bible *plain* to the common people instead of introducing into lessons "the melancholy jargon" of critics.

A similar defensive spirit pervaded the response to the American metropolis and its religious needs. Almost all populists have some exception in mind in their praise of the "people" and Sunday school leaders did not break the pattern. Like Theodore Frelinghuysen in the 1850s, they were appalled by the new immigrants washing up on the New World shore. "Now it is well known to our American delegates," said one U.S. speaker at the 1889 World Sunday School Convention in London, "that the city of New York is not an American city.... We would be glad if a great many more [immigrants] came from England than from other parts, because we have a great many with us whom we cannot call brethren." The "un-American" cities gave the Sunday school its most severe challenge as the century ended. An Iowan, raising the question of the frontier's location, said Sunday school discussions in his area were turning to the missionary grounds of the East and to the pressing issue, "How shall we evangelize Chicago? How shall we aid her in the suppression of anarchy? Or rather, in the suspension of anarchy at the end of a rope?"[21]

The frontier had shifted to the cities. A veteran worker in New York was sure the "Anarchist" had three Sunday schools of his own in Chicago and would soon have some in Manhattan, teaching men to hate God and their fellows.

The changing city seemed hostile and could not be accepted as a natural habitat by most Sunday school workers, who in a paradoxical way must have felt much like the newcomers disembarking on Ellis Island, lonely aliens on foreign soil.

Late nineteenth-century Sunday school leadership was no less awkward in efforts to help black Sunday schools. They tried any number of black-oriented experiments in the 1890s and 1900s. The International Convention hired black staff members to develop parallel organizational structures, that is, conventions at state and local levels, among the "colored people." Later, foundations and white workers sponsored special programs in black teacher training across the South. These tactics were largely unsatisfactory. The top echelon in the movement could never shake a feeling of guilt about their continuing failure to aid black Sunday schools. That failure reflected the vast chasm between black and white America.

The B. F. Jacobs forces were unable to discern or appreciate the unique contribution of the black Sunday school in those crucial years after the Civil War. In the South, for example, Sunday classes for blacks often had to take over the task of teaching reading and writing. As one black Sunday school veteran tried to tell the International Convention in 1881, Sunday instruction served as the "common school" of his people. Carter Woodson, one of the first historians of Negro education in America, had a similar impression about the important role black Sunday schools filled in bringing literacy to the recently freed slaves.

While all who have studied the subject lack extensive firsthand sources, it was Woodson's speculation that many blacks were able after emancipation to do openly what had been only covertly possible before: learn to read and write on Sunday—first learning the alphabet, then small words, and finally reading the Bible. The compelling motive, Woodson said, was for a "better knowledge of one's Christian duty and the reward awaiting the faithful. *Many of these Negroes often learned more on a single Sunday than the average student acquired in a day school during a week.*"[22]

Black colleges in the South, once they were started after the Civil War, seem to have sometimes included Sunday schools in which the faculty would teach. The colleges frequently had black congregations as bases and teachers understood when hired that they had responsibility in both college and Sunday school. The latter was designed to reach youths who could not qualify for the higher academic program. Both Woodson's theory and the links between black colleges and Sunday teaching indicated that the black Sunday school had its own distinctive work to do in the late nineteenth century. The elaborate paraphernalia of the white Sunday school convention was mostly irrelevant—a fact which the evangelical organizers did not clearly understand.

A leadership vacuum, the challenges of the city and the black Sunday schools—these were the big problems. But most irritating of all was the growing ridicule of the Sunday school. It was trivial but deflating. Earlier in the nineteenth century the critics had been apprehensive about the movement's strength and vitality; by the 1890s, however, fewer of them were willing to take it seriously. A crop of disdainful phrases appeared in everyday speech: innocent as a Sunday school picnic, naïve as Sunday school faith, sincere as a Sunday school voice. Mark Twain had fun with the last phrase in his account of how Tom Sawyer beat the system of memorizing Bible verses. Mr. Walters, Tom's Sunday school superintendent, "was very earnest of mien, and very sincere and honest at heart; and he held sacred things and places in such reverence, and so separated them from worldly matters, that unconsciously to himself his Sunday-school voice had acquired a peculiar intonation which was wholly absent on weekdays."[23]

Some humor was light. "When is a school not a school?" Answer, "When it's a Sunday school." And then there was a savage kind. In the fall of 1900 John D. Rockefeller, Jr., became leader of the Men's Bible Class of the Fifth Avenue Baptist Church in New York City, succeeding Charles Evans Hughes, later Chief Justice of the U.S. Supreme Court. The new teacher soon attracted all manner of attention from the newspapers, partly because the name Rockefeller symbolized everything that outraged them about American business and partly because the Sunday school was ripe for jest. "With his hereditary grip on a nation's pocketbook," said the *Pittsburgh Press,* "his talks on spiritual matters are a tax on piety." Cartoonists had a field day. The New York *Journal* depicted Rockefeller in front of his class holding a Bible, tickertape spewing from his mouth."[24] The caption read, "The Modern Sunday School." Sunday schools had become highly visible, perhaps more visible and vulnerable than the "Illinois Band" had bargained for.

Even so, a "last hurrah" for the era of Jacobs and his group was heard in Washington, D.C. in 1910 at the World's Sixth Sunday School Convention. None other than President William Howard Taft addressed the global conclave, assuring delegates that, "No matter what views are taken of general education, we all agree—Protestant, Catholic and Jew alike—that Sunday-school education is absolutely necessary to secure moral uplift and religious spirit." Taft's words, which may have offfended Catholics and Jews, were an unwitting portent of pluralism and the vagueness of American religion in the twentieth century.

But in 1910 a glorious past could be enjoyed in momentary relaxation about the future. Congress adjourned so members could walk in the grand parade, a festive occasion despite a heavy downpour of rain. Spectators along the routes glimpsed such banners as "The Saloon Must Go," "Justice [David Josiah] Brewer was a Sunday School Teacher," "The Men of America for the Man of Galilee," and "Taft is Square on the Sunday School." A rousing booster spirit abounded in special yells from the various delegations as they passed the reviewing stand:

> Colorado is big, Colorado is great,
> We are the only centennial state;
> We have gold in our mines; we have silver galore,
> We have money in banks and goods in our stores;
> But the brightest assets in our glorious state
> Are the workers for God that our Sunday schools make.

The most touching gesture of all was the song of the Illinois delegation:

Not without thy wondrous glory, / Illinois, Illinois,
Can be writ the nation's glory, / Illinois, Illinois,
On the record of thy years / Dwight L. Moody's name appears,
Jacobs, Reynolds and our tears, / Illinois, Illinois.

It was a poignant appeal to the glories of the past. Moody and Reynolds—these two comrades who had made a pact in 1864 to capture a state Sunday school convention—had answered their last roll call; so had Generalissimo Jacobs. Even though world and North American Sunday school conventions would continue for many decades, in 1910 a dream was fading. It was the end of an era.

Notes

1. Andrew Mills, op. cit., p. 104. Reynolds' remark about the Sunday school as the "cream" of the church was recorded in *Official Report of the Tenth International Sunday School Convention* (1902), p. 233.

2. Simeon Gilbert, *The Lesson System* (New York: Phillips and Hunt, 1879), p. 26.

3. H. Wayne Morgan, "Toward National Unity," *The Gilded Age,* revised edition (ed.) H. Wayne Morgan (Syracuse: Syracuse University Press, 1970), p. 2.

4. Henry F. May, *Protestant Churches and Industrial America* (New York: Harper & Row, 1967), p. 77.

5. Daniel J. Boorstin, *The Americans: The National Experience* (New York: Random House, 1965), p. 121.

6. Francis J. McConnell, *By The Way* (New York: Abingdon-Cokesbury Press, 1952), p. 233.

7. Gilbert, op. cit., p. 37.

8. Ibid., p. 46.

9. *Eighth International Sunday School Convention* (1896), p. 252.

10. *Official Report of the Tenth International Sunday School Convention* (1902), pp. 166, 167.

11. *Ninth International Sunday School Convention* (1899), p. 92.

12. *The Autobiography of William Allen White* (New York: The Macmillan Company, 1946), p. 44.

13. *First International Sunday School Convention* (1875), pp. 45, 47.

14. Shailer Mathews, *New Faith for Old* (New York: The Macmillan Company, 1936), p. 245.

15. *Sixth International Sunday School Convention* (1890), pp. 169-70.

16. Thomas Curtis Clark, "An Estimate of the International Sunday School Convention," *The Christian Century* (XXXI, July 9, 1914).

17. *Offical Report of the Tenth International Sunday School Convention* (1902), p. 224.

18. *Seventh International Sunday School Convention* (1893), p. 178.

19. *Eighth International Sunday School Convention* (1896), p. 178.

20. *Ninth International Sunday School Convention* (1899), p. 35.

21. *Fifth International Sunday School Convention* (1887), p. 82.

22. Carter Godwin Woodson, *The History of the Negro Church* (Washington, D.C.: The Associated Publishers, 1921), p. 268. Italics added.

23. Mark Twain, *The Adventures of Tom Sawyer* (New York: Grosset and Dunlap, 1946), p. 39.

24. Raymond B. Fosdick, *John D. Rockefeller, Jr.: A Portrait* (New York: Harper & Brothers, 1956), pp. 126-27.

CHAPTER 6

Old-Time School vs. New-Time School

We might as well admit it; the Sunday school is dead.[1]
—a church professional

The Sunday school is the "most indispensable institution in America."[2]
—an "old-timer"

A few conscientious observers at the world Sunday school parade in 1910 would happily have sung "Shall We Gather at the River?" one last time and laid the "Army of the Lord" to rest in Arlington National Cemetery. Announcements of the imminent or late demise of the Sunday school movement began when the twentieth century was budding and have continued with regularity since. In truth, the Washington gathering was one of the movement's last superspectaculars; chief executives since President Taft have not often extolled it as necessary for

117

national moral uplift nor has Congress adjourned for Sunday school parading. But neither has the institution vanished, despite the fact that the twentieth-century Sunday school epic has contained no particularly noteworthy personalities, no heroics. Compared to the nineteenth century, the story is bland. Yet there is drama, the drama of how an institution judged passé by the "better" critics and professional theorists refused to die.

Criticism of all schools is a recurring American pastime, but none has been so savagely attacked since 1900 as the Sunday school. Assaults upon public schools usually arouse a vigorous defense from well-known, influential persons. The admirers of the Sunday school, however, have gone largely unheard in the midst of the chorus of detractors. One of the foremost Protestant educators of the 1920s doubted that Sunday instruction could ever recover a genuine educational purpose since, he said, the traditions, the unpaid teaching force, the lack of standards, the curriculum and the clergy were all "against it."[3]

The outmoded Sunday school, so its critics have proposed, should be replaced by weekday ecumenical programs, study *about* religion in public schools, released-time programs, family-centered instruction, or vacation church schools. Name changes have seemed advisable on numerous occasions. Early in the century the label "church school" was put forth to avoid the "repellent" overtones of the past. That name was adopted by some denominations; the Methodists in local churches of the 1940s had virtual pitched battles between "church school" and "Sunday school" devotees, with the former winning in official policy. Others have preferred to call it "the Sunday morning session of the school of the Church."

When the ailing patient did not die before mid-century, John Wanamaker's pet institution became the object of that hostility that human beings reserve for the dying. In the 1940s it was variously described as a "menace," or an "hour of charm."[4] Charles Clayton Morrison, the renowned editor of *The Christian Century,* found the Sunday school a convenient scapegoat for all sorts of skulduggery. He accused the single weekly hour led by volunteer teachers of causing a downward curve in religious literacy and respect for religion. Shaking his finger at the Sunday school, Morrison moaned that "American society has become a secular-minded society."[5]

If there is cognizance of such things on the bank of the "river that flows by the throne of God," a company of the saints who wrote Sunday school obituaries are probably embarrassed, for it has outlived them, and in a relatively unreformed state has outlived a host of reformers. The folkways of popular religion are never easily altered, but the grip of habit and custom only partly explains why the old-time Sunday school has persisted despite its death notices. As inherited, the cause has remained a lively one for millions of Christians who have refused in the twentieth century to abandon a treasured institution without a struggle.

The ensuing fight became symbolic of a deep split within American Protestantism. On one side were the church *professionals,* a new breed ready and determined to reform Sunday school in accordance with changing dictates of modern culture. From the early years of the twentieth century to the 1940s the professional banner was carried by the "religious educators." The next generation—the postliberal church educators and their successors—continued the professionals' fight after World War II. On the other side was a shifting array of opposing forces. Most obvious were the *old-timers,* the evangelicals who wanted to keep the Sunday school much as it was in the days of B. F.

Jacobs. In addition, many laymen maintained a quiet but steady underground resistance against the reformers. The lengthy conflict shaped up more like the entrenched snarling along the Hindenburg line in World War I than the decisive Allied route at El Alamein in World War II. Timetables have varied from place to place and sniper fire is still heard today. Of course, inertia has figured in the story as a force often playing into the hands of old-timers. These modern tensions over the Sunday school reveal much more about the multi-layered nature of Protestant culture than do historical approaches sampling only the currents in theologies, denominational politics and ecumenical strata.

"Middletown," 1910–1945: The Disappointment of the Professionals

Henry Seidel Canby, once editor of *The Saturday Review of Literature,* remembered Sunday school in the 1890s as a time of "Bible stories parroted by misses doing their duty, and of a catechism as meaningless in that untheological age as a treatise on alchemy, yet memorized and re-memorized." Many youngsters had similar experiences, because Sunday school was not a school in any acceptable meaning of the word so much as an integral part of a unique and forgotten set of activities forming the Victorian Sabbath. The fabric of that day had many strands: church, Sunday school, special clothes; roast beef and the Sunday newspaper for more casual families; and cold meat, hymn sings, Bible reading and peaceful walks for stricter households. The day was extraordinary. "For with clean collar and cuffs and a Sunday suit, one put on decorum," Canby recalled, "and in the calm of the quiet neigborhood the mind relaxed, and when the bells began, the slow march of so many church-goers ranged by families, and dressed for a rite, stirred in the consciousness a sense of immemorial ... custom."[6]

Sharing the same memory but not relishing it were the religious educators, a new generation in a different world from that of B. F. Jacobs. They were college-trained, attracted to the progressive spirit of John Dewey in education and the Social Gospel of Walter Rauschenbusch in theology, and unafraid of the latest scholarly judgment of biblical critics. This able, up-to-date crowd wanted, above all, a religion appealing to like-minded moderns. Obviously, the old Sunday school would no longer do; whatever the other disagreements of the religious educators, they agreed on that point. The new breed respected the dedicated volunteers, the "misses doing their duty," but entertained no nostalgia about Sunday school as part and parcel of immemorial custom. After all, the progressives reasoned, the institution was barely over a hundred years old and already stale and irrelevant; it represented the wrong kind of permanence in a rapidly changing society. The Sunday school had to be reformed.

In passing, it should be said that the reformers frequently turned to Horace Bushnell, the nineteenth-century liberal, for support, and they appropriated that intellectual giant in a historically peculiar way. Bushnell contributed little to the Sunday school movement in his day, 1802–1876, for his contention that children should be raised as if they had always been Christian flew in the face of Sunday school ideology in the mid-nineteenth century when youngsters were treated as "little adults needing conversion." By appealing to Bushnell within a Sunday school context, religious educators gave their reforming ideas an undeserved appearance of maturity. They also created the impression, which too few historians have bothered to correct, that Bushnellian "Christian nurture" was an integral part of popular Protestant education.

Uniform lessons were a special symbol of the old-fashioned way. The plan violated the religious educators' common sense and their psychological views; it was educational absurdity to subject persons of different ages to the same lesson. What a child understands and *needs*—a new word soon turned into a cliché in the lexicon of Protestant education—was not always fitting for adults, they claimed. Even more, what makes sense to adults is often mystifying and bewildering to small children. Such criticism of the uniform lessons was not without substance: in the fall of 1906 a four-year-old boy started his Christian schooling with a lesson on the problem of whose wife a woman would be in the resurrection when she had married seven men. Furthermore, the Bible was badly mangled. Old Testament lesson favorites, picked because they presumably interested youngsters, were Joseph, David, and Daniel in the lions' den, while prophets got short shrift except for occasional temperance sessions plucked out of Amos. Willard Uphaus, the peace radical and a religious educator in the 1920s, put his finger on a real weakness of uniform lessons. He noted that the hopping and skipping from one part of the Bible to another gave children little chance to "comprehend the long-time historical development . . . of the ethical and religious concepts being taught them. . . ."[7]

Further, religious educators charged that traditional curriculum neglected the interests and affections of adolescents. Here was a fairly new concern. The notion of adolescense as a separate stage of life did not emerge until the latter part of the nineteenth century. Teenagers gained the spotlight only after education for industrial society gradually lengthened the time spent in school and, consequently, postponed full adult responsibility. Protestants in the 1880s and 1890s introduced questions still in vogue today: Can the church "hold on" to teenagers? Can sexual potency be contained during that increasingly long stretch between puberty and marriage? Both questions bothered the imaginations of Sunday educators.

Organizations to meet the *needs* of adolescents came into the picture. One model was Christian Endeavor, founded in 1881 by a Congregational minister in Portland, Maine, but the denominations were not willing to let too much money or energy be squandered on interdenominational outfits. The Methodist Epworth League and the Baptist Young People's Union of America were started by 1889. Well into the twentieth century, countless new adult-inspired efforts to capture the attention of youth were set in motion, using passwords, secret formulas, uniforms, membership badges, and rafts of officers. The ancient ideal of knighthood inspired several groups. Knights of the Holy Grail had as its motto, "Confession, Chastity, Charity."

None of this quite stilled the anxiety and edginess of church fathers about the challenges presented by teenagers. Sunday school publications in the twentieth century's first quarter were filled with warnings against "poolroom habits," admonitions to boys not to think about sex, and attacks on the "degrading" teachings of the street. The 1911 International Sunday School Convention introduced a Department of Purity to instill the ideals of the "white life," a Victorian euphemism for sexual abstinence. Religious educators were sympathetic to these initiatives but knew the Sunday school had a long way to go in dealing adequately with adolescents.

Basically, the reformers were embarrassed by Sunday school ineptitude as an educational venture. Public schools overshadowed the church programs, whose progressive edges were few and whose most visible symbols of back-wardness were its facilities. Quarters were often nothing more than the church basement, those "cold, gloomy underground rooms delicately frescoed with furnace pipes."[8] Or if a nineteenth-century congregation could afford an educational "plant," it was usually modeled on the Akron plan—a cavernous theater with the superintendent's desk on the stage and partitioned alcoves for classes around the edge of the auditorium. The Akron design, first used in that Ohio city, was considered the best form for any school featuring uniform lessons: the superintendent could conduct the opening exercises, keep an eye on classes and then review the lesson at the close, all from the lofty splendor of his desk. By 1910 most "new Sunday school buildings had encased the outmoded uniform lesson plan in expensive brick and mortar. The remains of that enthusiasm dot the land today, but the stages have come in handy for congregations trying to "hold on" to teenagers through drama ministries.

Mortifying to the religious educators was the gimmick-ridden appeal of the average Sunday program. The old-timers had resorted to a variety of promotional techniques to sustain and increase their booming enterprise. A loyal Sunday school army was a popular way of maintaining attendance and discipline: "On Time Every Time, A Learned Lesson Every Time, and An Offering for Christ Every Time." An "On Timer's Tribe" had a "pledge to bind and a pin to remind." Local schools had rally days, decision days, children's days, concerts and picnics. National organizations abounded for each age group with headquarters, mottos and special songs.

The religious educators looked upon this hustle and bustle as empty efforts of well-intentioned workers, amateurs who had too long dominated the Sunday school.

Amateurism was, in fact, the nub of their quarrel with the traditional movement. *Professional* leadership must take over. And why not? Experts were evident in public schools, social work and municipal life. Should Protestant education be different? Volunteer leaders, in the reformers' scheme, should be aided by a full-time "director of religious education" if a congregation could afford one. If not, the minister was expected to assume the mantle of the professional. At the very least a specialist should be at work in every state and denominational center. The formula was straightforward: no professional, no reform; no school worthy of respect.

Few groups were more insistent upon that formula than the independent Religious Education Association formed in 1903 at the instigation of President William Rainey Harper of the University of Chicago. A man of many talents, Harper had a long-standing interest in popularizing the scholarly study of scripture. His pioneering work on biblical correspondence courses was, in part, a flank attack upon the uniform lessons. So, too, was the creation of the Association. Its founders included some of the most illustrious names in university and religious life at the turn of the century. This small agency developed into a "brain trust" for the reformers who hoped to transform the Sunday school into a thoroughly modern institution.

If the Association was the "brain trust," the International Council of Religious Education was the organizing center of the updating movement. The Council, founded in 1922, was a single expression of both the Sunday school convention heritage and the concerns of powerful denominational boards of education. It represented the aspiring professional's best chance for a major breakthrough. Within the Council a staff of well-trained educators laid out ambitious plans for sweeping changes in the curricular diet of Sunday schools. Their proposed "International curriculum" was far more than just a replacement for the old-style uniform lesson plan; it was to embody the latest findings in education. The era of "graded lessons" had finally arrived, after long years of preparation.

Graded lessons depended on the insights and theories of such men as John Dewey, William James and E. L. Thorndike whose approaches became pervasive in public education during the early twentieth century. Foremost was the necessity to take account of motivation, stages of maturity and gradations of learning ability. Small, successive steps were deemed more appropriate in the learning process than full and repeated exposure to a whole corpus of information. Taking seriously the developmental needs of each age group, religious educators prepared Sunday school materials and teaching guides for infants, toddlers, primary elementary pupils, older elementary children, junior high school youngsters, senior highs, older youths, young married adults, mature adults and senior adults. Pleasant physical surroundings conducive to learning at each particular age were recommended. Cribs, three or four sizes of ribbed-back Sunday school chairs for children, and classroom decorative material appeared in supply catalogs.

To their credit, religious educators imbued with Deweyan psychology pushed beyond the Akron plan in church school facilities. They were often successful in persuading congregations that learning was enhanced by settings more comfortable and functional than auditoriums with partitioned cubbyholes. The reformers were most adventurous in organizing a farflung program in teacher training. At least for a while the Sunday school teachers seemed almost abreast of public school counterparts in exposure to the latest and best educational thinking.

For all their new-found expertise, the religious educators were never able to generate the kind of mass enthusiasm which prevailed in the golden days of the nineteenth century. At that time the visible leaders of the movement had been laymen such as B. F. Jacobs and John Wanamaker. By 1930, however, the old-style volunteers had been eased out of seats on top-level boards supposedly directing Sunday school affairs. The full-time professional was clearly in charge and the volunteers were treated, perhaps unconsciously, as potential trainees, the beneficiaries of the experts' guidance. Local teachers—laymen— resented the apparent condescension from on high.

Then, too, the religious educators' version of progressivism was abstract and vaguely unsettling to the mass of workers. In the old days the purpose of teaching was reasonably clear: conversion. For instance, when the senior Rockefellers settled in New York and took up Sunday school labors along the Hudson, Mrs. Rockefeller kept track of her pupils by listing their names in a notebook, with a capital C before those who were orthodox Christians. After one name she added this note, "Died July 2, 1894, the first to go and not a Christian."[9] Mrs. Rockefeller's evangelical certainty was not shared by twentieth-century religious educators who tended to indulge in blurry talk of "righteous living" and Christian "character education"—goals difficult to translate into classroom practicalities for teachers who spent only two or three hours per week on Sunday school matters. Similarly, the methods of progressive education—the experience-centered approach with a stress on problem-solving and attention to student needs—required a sophistication and commitment of time unavailable among rank-and-file vol-unteers.

Not surprisingly, religious educators were poorly re-ceived in the hinterlands, and also rather coolly welcomed by fellow professionals in the public sector. Was all the fuss about religious education necessary when public schools were doing so well in the formation of character? "In its earlier stages," Shailer Mathews bitingly commented, "re-ligious education was secular education dressed in a Prince Albert coat."[10]

Meanwhile, the life of the ordinary Sunday school went on much as it had, routines and customs changing little. B. F. Jacobs would have felt right at home in most classes in the 1920s, especially in "Middletown," that typical Ameri-can community made famous by Robert and Helen Lynd in their epoch-making sociological study. The Lynds re-ported some variations between schools and modest im-provements here and there, but for the most part, they said, "going to Sunday School is much the same sort of activity in all classes and in all churches and has changed relatively little since the nineties." The Lynds' description of an average Sunday school included everything the reli-gious educators disliked:

A noisy earnestness characterizes the opening exercises, punctuated with much bustling to and fro by late-comers and secretaries. Hymns are sung lustily, especially the favorites with repeated choruses such as "I'm going to go to glory by and by." During the prayers of the superintendent adults may utter fre-quent "Amens," while restless children stare about or idly pinch each other. The whole school listens to the reading of the lesson, after which it breaks up into little groups scattered through the room, each with an earnest teacher leaning over the back of the pew in front, facing his class... [about thirty minutes later classes are] interrupted by a bell from the platform, and the superintendent asked for "anybody wishing to leave a message"; there being no answer, the collection was announced, school papers distributed, and the school clattered out into the sunshine.[11]

Judged by religious educators' standards, the Sunday school in "Middletown" was a disaster. While hundreds of similar communities filled the countryside, the reformers could point to few models embodying their ideology.

Give Me That "Old-Time" School: 1910–1945

Soon after the Wall Street crash of 1929, the professionals could have begun preparing for defeat at the grass roots. First, the depression erased many traces of their reformist activity, mainly because they lost the battle of the budget. Professional workers cost money, but the old-style Sunday school was inexpensive as well as durable. Then came the blow of a new theology seeping in from Europe in the 1930s and 1940s. Religious educators had hooked their cause to liberal theology, in America a blend of historical progressivism and the Social Gospel. The new theology, stemming from such figures as Karl Barth and Reinhold Niebuhr, enjoyed a period of popularity during which liberalism was discredited.

Next, the reformers' image of the future proved too optimistic. They anticipated a future of slow but unending progress just as they believed in the possibility of continual growth for each individual—a persuasion typical of that idealistic generation whose formative years came around the turn of the century. Many Americans of that time, as one interpreter has put it, saw "the main guarantee of universal morality . . . neither in the mind of God nor in argument nor in tradition, but in the *unfolding American future."*[12] Actually, the goal they held was not vastly different from Lyman Beecher's desire to reconcile national prosperity with purity and future blessedness. Hope in America's future provided the courage to take on the complex task of remaking a well-established institution, carving out a new profession and reforming popular religious opinions. It was admittedly an audacious task for a small band of seminary professors, church bureaucrats and their followers. If the original Sunday school backers, relatively few, could attract an aroused constituency, why not the religious educators? They thought they could gather troops, and expected a mass movement based on American common sense. Even more important, they presupposed that people are pragmatic, mentally alert and steeped in democratic love. Children are innately curious, intelligent, healthy-minded persons who would someday help remake the world. Therein, they thought, lay the hope of the future.

Sadly for the hopeful, twentieth-century America experienced a different kind of progress, full of ironic twists and unexpected consequences. Totally unexpected by the religious educators was the final and major reason for their decline: they simply failed to attract the needed recruits, and they alienated nonprofessional evangelicals who elected to remain outsiders to the world of scholarship, relevance and social action. Although the reformers believed firmly in democracy, they impressed opponents as another elite group trying to force their will upon the people. Staunchly against any form of clerical domination or authoritarianism in religion, they were nonetheless accused of being a new "priestly class," professionals who thought they knew what was best for others. The outreach was to all people, particularly the working class and neglected urban children. But that also failed; their gospel proved more acceptable to the middle class, people much like the reform leaders themselves.

Almost from the start of the twentieth century the hard-working amateurs of the traditional Sunday school suspected that the university-trained experts were trying to take the "college of the common people" away from those it was meant to serve. Pride mingled with earnest conviction in the old-timer who lashed out at "pretentious gentlemen" rushing into print and onto platforms to find fault with "the plain yeomanry who come from factory and office and farm, and take boys and girls an hour a week with no other compulsion than that of love, and with little other preparation than the love of God's Book and the hope to make it an instrument of salvation to those whom they teach. . . . We have done, and are doing, a great work. The education we give is that of the heart, not the head."[13]

"Heart" and "head" once again became rival symbols. Yet whereas in church education of the nineteenth century the mind had been relegated to second place in the scale of values, the twentieth-century distinction sent the two in opposite directions within the Sunday school itself. The polarizing of heart and head was an old-timer's way of using populism against specialists. But it also meant the old-timers were turning their backs on certain intellectual and social trends at work in the culture. They relinquished their claim to an impact on the whole of American life. This, at least, was a consequence which the evangelicals seemingly had to accept to save their Sunday schools.

The crucial decade for the old-timers was the 1920s. American culture was going modern; a new mentality was celebrated in advertising, in national magazines, and on the radio. Growing, sophisticated urban styles left little room for the "better values" of old America. Small-town and rural Protestants were prepared to fight a battery of enemies—intellectual secularists, religious modernists, Catholics and minorities. The Ku Klux Klan, Prohibitionism, opposition to evolution, and the underground campaign against the Presidential candidacy of Al Smith, a Catholic, were part of that struggle. A lasting victory was scored in the restriction of immigration and a momentary one in Prohibition; but the old forces were losing on the broad scene and ultimately lost the war for censorship and against more casual manners and morals.[14]

No less threatening to the old-timers was what they saw happening in the Sunday school organizations. It was bad enough that the churches of their forefathers had warmed to liberalism. Worse yet was the way newcomers were capturing the crucial Sunday school spots. In the first thirty years of the century, denominational boards of education quietly shifted toward new operational styles, carried out by staff specialists. While few of the new men were outright biblical modernists, they talked and acted like professionals, as did the staff of the International Council of Religious Education. More was at stake than theological differences. Social and political heritages were also on the line. Fearing the end of the movement, old-timers cried out in pain; they mourned a past free of those they saw as bland experts dealing slights and snubs to the untutored. An unprecedented sort of class warfare emerged, an exercise in status politics which has become a mark of twentieth-century America. As much as financial empowerment and political success, it is *standing* which has motivated groups and individuals in the nation's brand of pluralism.

The evangelical Sunday school stalwarts did more than cry. They chose their ground, named the important work to do and refused to budge. They gave others the right to worry about the claims of the mind and, convinced that biblical scholars changed their views form day to day, turned indifferent ears to the latest opinion from the academic groves. Old-fashioned Sunday schools had no need of professors, proud scientists and new professionals who believed in the permanence of modern, liberal culture. The old-timers were not sure of the staying power of the world cherished by religious educators. The times were uncertain, and there were signs of God's coming judgment upon apostate churches and a sin-sick civilization. With a bleak future, why fret about relevance and being up to date? Two verities remained constant: the Bible as the Word of God and the Sunday lesson to teach that unchanging Word. As the nation moved into World War II, the old-timers' Sunday school was still seeking conversions.

Orthodoxy Meets Neo-Orthodoxy (1945-)

On the eve of the war, the Sunday schools in mainline denominations, which for the most part had plugged into the professional education circuit, were clearly in trouble. Enrollments had been slipping for years. Between 1926 and 1936 the Methodists reported a drop of 34 per cent; Disciples of Christ fell 23 per cent and Presbyterians, U.S.A. (Northern) 18 per cent. In contrast, sects and conservative groups were growing. The Assembly of God Sunday school increased its rolls by more than 300 per cent in the same decade, and the Pentecostal Holiness schools doubled their membership.

At this low ebb for the professionals, a transfusion was in the offing; a new group of postliberal educators appeared shortly after the war to fill the role played earlier by the religious education movement. The fervor created in denominational boards of Christian education and in the National Council of Churches (one of whose founding partners in 1950 was the International Council of Religious Education) again overshadowed the plodding and productive constancy of old-time evangelicals. In fact, post-World War II America was in the grips of such a massive religious revival that streams of enthusiasm were difficult to sort out.

The changing of the professional guard was heralded by the appearance in 1948 of the neo-orthodox "Faith and Life" series of the Presbyterian Church, U.S.A. The "new curriculum," as it was known throughout the 1950s, was a stunning success, both as a fresh breeze in the musty recesses of the Sunday school world and as a profitable publishing venture. Other denominations soon followed with revamped educational programs. The 1950s was the great decade for curricular innovation and renovation. Denominational boards and their printing facilities were hives of activity. And there was, in those years of the Eisenhower Administration, a momentary upswing of interest in mainline denominational Sunday schools.

Neo-orthodoxy was the major catalyst which helped to give the professionals new vigor. This theology in America reflected Calvinism as revitalized in Europe by Emil Brunner and Karl Barth, reinforced by Reinhold Niebuhr's assertion of the doctrine of original sin. It refuted the liberal reliance on progress, electing instead to emphasize God's sovereignty and the decisive revelation of the Bible. With liberal religious education already going stale in America, the new theology was an attractive option for enlivening Sunday schools.

Not all the programs in the 1950s were as unabashedly neo-orthodox as the Presbyterian's "Faith and Life" literature. Yet each did reflect, sooner or later, the new debate stimulated by theologians in the academic market place, and all were alike in at least two respects. First, they accepted the latest findings of biblical scholars, though that may not have been unmistakably clear to their audiences. Second, the curriculum revision was, by and large, the work of professionals who wanted to combine the best of theology and modern education.

Neo-orthodoxy had evangelical qualities but it was not identical with evangelical *orthodoxy*. It was much more attuned to the winds of modernity. As much as the postliberal educators might disagree theologically with their liberal predecessors, they still retained the professional stance—an eagerness to popularize current thought emanating from seminary and university, serious respect for the discoveries of professionals in the field of psychology, a drive for relevance, a zeal for public issues and an imperative to engage in social action. Catching up with Sunday school trends, *Time* magazine reported in late 1962 that "no longer does a teacher go into class armed only with the Good Book and a supply of patience built up over the previous six days. He is likely to have a skeleton text, a book of suggested activities, a visual-aid kit, and the advice of a child psychologist."[15]

As might have been expected, the postliberals found themselves in the same sort of trouble with their constituencies as did the religious educators. The new material was sometimes difficult to understand and hard for teachers to use despite a surge of training sessions. Besides, it mixed religion and politics. "Why can't we have something like they used in the good old days?" became a common plaintive plea.

The postliberals were no more successful than the liberals in scotching what seemed to sophisticated minds to be bizarre methods of enhancing Sunday school enrollment. For example, in the fall of 1952, cowboy actor Roy Rogers and his horse Trigger put in an appearance at the Trinity Methodist Church of Los Angeles. Rogers noted that it was

Trigger's first time to go to Sunday school. The San Ga-
briel (California) Union Church released helium-filled bal-
loons with tracts attached to lure residents to Sunday instruction. One stunt-conscious superintendent turned
himself into a modern Simeon Stylites, staying up in a
eucalyptus tree for twenty hours to evoke pledges of Sunday school attendance from sympathetic witnesses.

Throughout the neo-orthodox period the new generation upholding the nineteenth century evangelical spirit
remained quietly optimistic about the prospects for maintaining the old forms of Sunday school belief and practice.
Recruits for the old-timers' cause still looked to the institution as a crucial bulwark for evangelical faith. That same
1962 article in *Time* which observed the Sunday school
teacher's dependency on child pyschology also said:

Noting that 85 percent of the baptisms in his denomination
come by way of Sunday school, one Southern Baptist concludes
that "the greatest technique of evangelism in the twentieth century is not revivalism but the Sunday school."[16]

Old-timers could take comfort in the rapid growth of
Sunday schools outside the mainline churches. While
specialists plied their magic among standard brand denominations, the less ecumenical churches, Pentecostals
and other "fringe" groups, were on the move. The hand-
writing on the wall was coming clear by the early 1960s.
Denominations inside the National Council could not
match the Sunday school growth of churches beyond the
reach of typical ecumenism and theological revisionism.
The most rapidly expanding churches were independent
and almost fundamentalist groups replete with, often
centered around, Sunday schools.

Living with Pluralism (1965 —)

The vogue of undiluted neo-orthodoxy in mainline Protestant theology and among the denominations' professional educators waned as the merry-go-round of theological change began to move faster in the mid-1960s. Publication of Harvey Cox's *The Secular City* signaled a new interest in "worldly" theology. No sooner had this perspective been incorporated into the curriculum of the mainline denominations than the needle of fashion swung unsteadily toward "death of God," "hope," "black theology," and "joy and celebration." Sunday school literature planners and writers became weary victims of cultural lag. Hoping to be current, the best they could do, given publication schedules, was to keep up with what was the rage a year or two before.

Civil rights, the religious antiwar movement, student protests, and the new visibility of sex in public media were felt in the Sunday school, often as controversies pitting old-timers against church members and leaders more open to social change. Protestant theology was in disarray, and there was actually no way for church educators to keep up on all the intellectual and social action fronts or to deal with the enormous quantity of educational proposals.

One result of the turbulence of the 1960s and early 1970s was the assertion by the professionals that diversity, not uniformity, is required for effective modern church education. Pluralism became the great new slogan. Protestantism, of course, has always been pluralistic. Pluralism has reigned within most denominations as well as among them. Yet never has there been as much glorification of pluralism, so much bowing at its shrine, as has taken place along the American mainline in recent years. Challenged by blacks and other minorities, women, homosexuals, and other liberationists, and criticized by both evangelicals and secularists, the mainline denominations have tried to embrace every ideology and form of theology.

A desire to accommodate a pluralistic constituency emerged in the early 1970s as one major motivation in professional church education. This trend quickly became evident in the mainline literature; for example, the materials of the United Methodist Church. A proudly American denomination with more internal racial diversity and less historic dogmatism than the other Protestant communions, the United Methodist Church can be used to epitomize the mainline response in an era of self-conscious pluralism.

Evangelical and liberal, conservative and permissive, and newly conscious of its racial minorities, the United Methodist General Conference of 1972 enthroned pluralism by adopting a quasi-confessional statement declaring: "No single creed or doctrinal summary can adequately serve the needs and intentions of United Methodists in confessing their faith or in celebrating their Christian experience."[17] The statement had perhaps unanticipated implications for United Methodist curriculum makers, who in the 1960s had devised an elaborate revision that took account of civil rights and the other currents of the day. After 1972 racial minorities and women would be assured of still greater influence on the church school literature. ("Church school" is the official designation for Sunday school in the United Methodist Church.) These groups did not represent unsurmountable challenges to the church school establishment. Much more troublesome were the conservative evangelicals within the denomination. United Methodist traditionalists reasoned that formal pluralism guaranteed them a slice of the curriculum pie. They beseiged the literature editors with demands for Bible study materials more in keeping with their views.

The upshot of the 1972 United Methodist statement, entitled "Our Theological Task," was a kind of curriculum potpourri—a little of this and a little of that—served up to the entire denomination. Instead of offering specific series with appeal for theological progressives and others for the evangelicals, the United Methodists mixed assorted theological viewpoints in the same series, even the same quarterlies. It was hardly surprising that the approach was controversial. One United Methodist newspaper reported:

While some argue that different theological positions from quarter to quarter or even in the same books create confusion, Dr. [Ewart] Watts [the chief church school editor] said "others say the approach exposes both teachers and students to the broad spectrum of theological belief that exists in the United Methodist Church and enables them to test and evaluate their own faith."[18]

While the United Methodist Church's particular brand of Sunday school pluralism was still emerging, the denomination in 1976 launched a special church school emphasis called "Decision Point: The Next 100 Years." Initially organized for a four-year period, this emphasis had three objectives:

(1) To nurture and deepen the commitment of persons to Christ and the church through Christian growth and understanding by participating in the church school;
(2) To improve the quality of teaching and learning in every United Methodist church school; and
(3) To increase the number of persons who attend and are enrolled in United Methodist church schools.[19]

On the third objective, the nation's second largest Protestant denomination had clearly reached a crisis point by the mid-1970s. Church school enrollment dropped from 5.9 million in 1970–71 to 4.6 million in 1976–77. Could the pluralism reflected in the new literature reverse the membership trend? If Dean Kelley's thesis on "why conservative churches are growing" can be applied to Sunday schools, the United Methodists have opted for the sure formula for further erosion of both its church school enrollment and the loyalty of its members. Kelley convincingly argues that strictness, not liberalizing pluralism, is a key factor in the growth of religious groups.[20]

Rather than go it alone a dozen of the fourteen denominations in Joint Educational Development (JED) decided to confront pluralism together through a new curriculum designated "Christian Education; Shared Approaches." Joint Educational Development was born in the 1960s as a kind of dialogue group among professional church educators, and it is to its credit that it could persuade so many denominations to buy into its shared approaches. The new curriculum appeared in late 1978 with at least the tacit endorsements of the Christian Church (Disciples of Christ), the Episcopal Church, the Evangelical Covenant Church, the Presbyterian Church in the United States, the Reformed Church in America, the United Church of Christ, the United Presbyterian Church, the United Church of Canada, the Presbyterian Church in Canada, the Moravian Church in America, the Cumberland Presbyterian Church, and the Church of the Brethren. Significantly, several of these sponsors are too evangelical to fit comfortably on the mainline. Each denomination pledged not to continue its own curriculum after supplies on hand were sold.

Like the United Methodist literature conceived after

1972, "Christian Education—Shared Approaches" was intended to cover all bases:

The joint venture is planned to satisfy both conservatives and liberals, little churches and big ones, modest as well as affluent enterprises, highly educated congregations and those of average education. The curricula are not doctrinal, not denominational; they contain something for everybody.[21]

Centered on the Bible, the ecumenical materials come in four packages. "Knowing the Word" is a latter-day version of the uniform lessons, covering Old and New Testaments in a six-year cycle for all age groups. It is content oriented. "Interpreting the Word," designed for Sunday and weekday use among children and youth, is planned to help Christians respond to the Bible. "Living the Word," for all ages and for groups of mixed ages, is focused on the Christian community. "Doing the Word," ungraded and for any setting, is aimed at helping persons develop commitment to mission and grapple with social issues.

"Christian Education—Shared Approaches" did not create a detectable stir in the Sunday school world when it rolled off the presses. Its day may come; then it may not. An early, reasoned, and credibly objective analyst found it "bland and unexciting, even timid, not likely to enliven or inform the lives of either teachers or students."[22] "Exciting," however, is not a necessary quality of effective Sunday school literature. More important in historical terms is the excitement that teachers and students bring to the materials, and any denomination trying to revitalize its Sunday schools by providing exciting curricula will probably fail. Sunday schools seem to thrive best today when the excitement—for conversion, for Christian character building, or whatever—is experienced locally.

Measured by national statistics, the Sunday school is at least faltering, perhaps fading, in many of the denominations taking part in Joint Educational Development. For example, membership in the Episcopal Sunday school declined from 737,801 in 1970–71 to 597,751 in 1976–77; in the United Church of Christ from 766,244 to 553,119 and in the United Presbyterian Church from 1.3 million to slightly more than one million. Yet in all these and other mainline churches, Sunday schools have remained vital in some congregations.

No single pattern accounts for local success in mainline Sunday schools. Some congregations apparently attract children and adults by clinging to traditional forms, others by introducing innovation and a third group by combining the old and the new. Decisions are often made on the basis of what works in a given place rather than through the guidance of either old-timers or the professionals, although some of the church educators have very practical and helpful suggestions to offer. Without knowing that Iris Cully had proposed the use of short-term teachers in a day when superintendents have trouble recruiting leaders for a full year,[23] one Presbyterian Sunday school in the Bronx hit upon the idea of organizing its courses of study in segments that can be handled by a series of teachers for a given class. That congregation no longer has a problem in recruiting teachers, who can volunteer for time periods as short as two weeks or as long as seven months, and its Sunday school fills up the available space.

While the mainline denominations have moved into the 1980s agonizing on their national levels about the future of Christian education vis à vis the Sunday school, the evangelical churches have pulled away from the slump they too feared they would enter in the early 1970s. The Southern Baptist Convention showed signs about 1970 of following the United Methodists and United Presbyterians into the downward Sunday school spiral. While national figures in 1976 showed only a 2.4 percent increase over 1965, the bicentennial year was the fifth in a row for a membership gain. An aggressive new Sunday school campaign initiated in 1976 produced seventeen hundred schools with an average enrollment of sixty persons each within two years.[24]

Other evangelical, as well as the Pentecostal and fundamentalist, denominations enlarged their Sunday schools in the 1970s. From what was once considered the Protestant fringes came the phenomena of gigantic Sunday schools—some with attendances of more than five thousand weekly—equaling, even surpassing, anything from the late nineteenth century. Most of the largest Sunday schools of the 1970s, as in the previous decade, were Independent Baptist, Southern Baptist, or affiliates of the Baptist Bible Fellowship. These schools boasted of hundreds of volunteer staff members and, usually, fleets of buses. Every one of the largest schools, said one investigator, was "led by an aggressive, gifted pastor, who heads up a militant program of evangelism."[25] Most of them also have set a pattern of developing their own curriculum, or of buying material from independent companies such as David C. Cook, Gospel Light Publications, and the Scripture Press, which offer Bible-centered, conversion-seeking literature.

The disparity of strength between old-timers' Sunday schools and those of ecumenically inclined denominations suggested in the period from 1965 into the 1980s that the leadership of the movement had already passed into the hands of custodians long ignored or rejected by establishment professionals. Certainly the evangelicals were convinced the shift had taken place, that the future again belonged to them. "Spiritual emphasis characterizes the 'new look' in evangelical Sunday schools," said one of their leaders as early as 1961. "There has been a complete break with the naturalistic and coldly intellectual approach in religious education and a turn to the warmly personal and experiential appeal. . . . Evangelicals see the Sunday school as a divine institution with divine oversight, a divine mission and a divine program."[26]

How different in many respects these old-timers' schools are from their predecessors in the days of B. F. Jacobs. But Jacobs, and certainly John Wanamaker, would have liked the fleets of Sunday school buses, the television outreach of many of the hundred largest schools of the 1970s and the zeal for telling the old, old story to children and adults on the Sabbath morning.

As the twentieth century moved into its ninth decade, many an evangelical stood up to cheer "the most indispensable institution in America."

Notes

1. Wesner Fallaw, "Now for the School of the Church!" *The Christian Century* (LXII, June 6, 1945), p. 676.
2. Clarence H. Benson, *A Popular History of Christian Education* (Chicago: Moody Press, 1943), p. 9.
3. George H. Betts, "If the Sunday School Fails," *The Christian Century* (XLII, January 29, 1925), p. 155.
4. Lockhart Amerman, "The Menace of the Sunday School," *The Christian Century* (LXI, February 9, 1944), p. 173.
5. Charles Clayton Morrison, "Protestantism and the Public School," *The Christian Century* (LXIII, April 17, 1946), p. 490.
6. Henry Seidel Canby, *American Memoir* (Boston: Houghton Mifflin Company, 1947), p. 68.
7. Willard Uphaus, *Commitment* (New York: McGraw-Hill Book Company, Inc., 1963), p. 28.

8. Franklin D. Elmer, "Recent Progress in the Sunday School," *Education and National Character* (Chicago: The Religious Education Association, 1908), p. 279.
9. Raymond B. Fosdick, op. cit., p. 24.
10. Shailer Mathews, op. cit., p. 249.
11. Robert and Helen S. Lynd, *Middletown* (New York: Harcourt, Brace and Co., 1929), pp. 391, 388–89.
12. Henry F. May, *The End of American Innocence* (Chicago: Quadrangle Books, 1964), p. 14. Italics added.
13. H. M. Hamill, "The Sunday-School as an Educational Force," *The Development of the Sunday School: 1780–1905* (Boston: The Executive Committee of the International Sunday School Association, 1905), p. 177.
14. Richard Hofstadter, *The Paranoid Style in American Politics and other Essays* (New York: Alfred A. Knopf, 1966), p. 78.
15. "Look Dad, I'm Leaving," *Time* (LXXX, December 7, 1962),
16. Ibid.
17. "Our Theological Task," *The Book of Discipline of the United Methodist Church* (Nashville: The United Publishing House, 1972), p. 80.
18. "U M Editor Defends 'Pluralism,'" *United Methodist Reporter* (VII, May 25, 1979), p. 4
19. *Decision Point: Church School* (Nashville: The Board of Discipleship of the United Methodist Church, undated), p. 1.
20. Dean Kelley, *Why Conservative Churches Are Growing* (New York: Harper & Row, 1972).
21. Phoebe M. Anderson, "Up and Down and 'Seesaw,'" *The Christian Century* (XCVI, March 21, 1979), p. 316.
22. Ibid.
23. "Future of Sunday School Is Tied to Adjustment to U.S. Realities," Religious News Service, April 23, 1976.
24. Figures cited by James Lackey, Southern Baptist Sunday School Board Growth Consultant, Religious News Service, September 14, 1978.
25. Elmer Towns, "America's Largest Sunday Schools are Growing," *Christian Life* (XXXII, August, 1970), p. 15.
26. James DeForest Murch, *Teach or Perish!* (Grand Rapids: William B. Eerdmans Publishing Company, 1961), p. 52.

CHAPTER 7

The Last Great Religious Movement?

*To internalize our history, we need once again to be-
come a story-telling people. We must find a way to tell
the story as our story. The old Sunday School took that
concern seriously. People knew and cared about the
story; it was theirs and they wanted to pass it on.* [1]

—JOHN WESTERHOFF

One staple in the reading diet of American high school
students in days gone by was Edgar Allan Poe's "The Purloined Letter," a short story with a twist to intrigue young
minds in the pretelevision world. A stolen document must
be hidden in a room that will be thoroughly searched.
Where could it be put? In a secret panel? In a hollowed-out
rung of a chair? The answer, of course, is to leave the
letter in an obvious place where the sophisticated police,
looking for drawers with false bottoms, would ignore it. As

146

the tale goes, the treasured letter was put where everyone could see it—and no one did.

So it is with the Sunday School. The institution has been a fixture on the American scene for such a long time that today it is overlooked by most scholars, who in essence are detectives searching the cultural heritage for realities to illumine past, present, and future. "As a church historian," Martin E. Marty has said, "I have always been amazed to see how little attention has been given to this basic institution by historians and scholars."[2] The "purloined letter" syndrome also prevails among sociologists and educators, including "new time" religious educators whose theories on instruction and learning self-consciously avoid the term "Sunday school"—"church school" is a favored circumlocution—even though they know that a school-like program on Sundays remains the most prevasive style of Protestant education.

This syndrome makes it difficult for contemporary observers to understand the Sunday school as a dynamic religious movement or to comprehend the enthusiasm and acclaim it evoked a century or so ago. Today it seems quaint that the Congress of the United States would adjourn so members could march in the parade of the 1910 convention of the World Sunday School Association, and that even a ferocious rainstorm did not dampen the spirits of the "loyal Sunday School army." It seems a memory of cultural imperialism to recall the climactic moment of that convention. Two Sunday school leaders, one American and one British, stood on the platform. Suddenly two other men raced up from the audience and draped the Union Jack around the shoulders of the leader from Britain and the Stars and Stripes around the American. In one of the most transparently innocent statements ever recorded in print, the American was moved to say, "We have honor for all the flags of this world, but.../under these two flags the Anglo-Saxon people have upon themselves the responsibility under God of being the big brother to all the other flags."[3]

Among the favorite institutions of the American-British "big brother" was the Sunday school, equipped by temperament and purpose to help the Anglo-Saxon race work its magic its persuasive wiles upon an unsuspecting world. And that was not seen by Sunday school supporters as imperialistic, not even paternalistic./It was a matter of God-given, patriotic duty; after all, the movement was imbued with a firm belief in the truth of Postmaster General John Wanamaker's declaration, "the Sunday school was not evolved—it was revealed."[4]

Adapting a Revelation

/Although it may have been revealed from on high, the Sunday school has also evolved over the better part of two centuries/ The adaptability of Robert Raikes' idea of a school on Sunday is one reason a movement was born and flourished./Evolution and adaptability also explain why the Sunday school is not necessarily a conscious or unconscious tool of Anglo-Saxon imperialism today/ For example, the black American denominations are strongly devoted to the Sunday school as an instrument for evangelism and for developing personal identifications with the biblical story. Moreover, with the advent of contemporary black theologies in the late 1960s, many black church leaders turned to the Sunday school as a suitable forum for inculcating a sense of liberation in black young people.

Even the white-dominated British-American movement has undergone several significant adaptations since the

1780s, and the ability of the big little school to change without losing its basic characters is one of its major strengths. Like its origin, the evolution of the Sunday school was directed in large part by changing social situations.

The Industrial Revolution had created havoc and disorder within English society in the latter half of the eighteenth century. As the older agriculturally-based society was uprooted, a flood of disoriented rural folk poured into the towns and cities, not unlike the more recent northward in-migration within the United States. These country folk, once they invaded the cities, became the unwitting victims of the factory system. Adults and children worked for a pittance. The institution of the Sabbath provided the only escape from relentless drudgery and routine. Sunday was a free day, and on that day hordes of children roamed the streets, disrupting civil order and creating mild chaos that unnerved the English gentry and merchants alike. As described in chapter 1, Raikes was touched by the spectacle of these ruffians who constantly flirted with trouble on the Sabbath. Along with a few other Anglican evangelicals—all laypersons—he launched what was probably the first Sunday "charity" school, an institution that provided a smattering of instruction in reading and in prayers.

The "charity" school was imported to America to meet a somewhat similar problem. Confusion and disorder reigned in many of the larger cities. Especially in New York City and Philadelphia, the first American Sunday schools were designed to preserve the sanctity of the Sabbath and to reach a group of neglected human beings. But once arrived on these shores, the "first day" school was soon converted by evangelical Protestants into an integral part of their distinctive pattern of education, a pattern organized around a network of interpenetrating institutions. The genius of the American people in the years from 1815 to 1860 was located not so much in persons as in institutions.

At the heart of the educational ecology of the evangelical Protestants was the *Revival*. Around this center clustered an array of enterprises, propelled into existence and maintained by a determination to convert the whole population. The Sunday school, as embodied by the American Sunday School Union, was one of the first offshoots of the Revival. Next came the nineteenth-century denominational college, an institution markedly different from its colonial predecessor. Then arose the theological seminary, an American creation. Also included in this ecology were the system of public schools beginning to take form, various voluntary associations, foreign and domestic mission agencies and a variety of reform movements, such as the abolition of slavery and the promotion of peace and temperance. Numerous religious journals kept church people informed about the accomplishments of each of these ventures.

That basic pattern is still in evidence, though often in a feeble and disordered state. The problems of the contemporary Sunday school are not simply those of one institution; they reflect a larger systemic confusion within the Protestant enterprise as a whole. But wherever the old ecology remains intact, and that is usually where the evangelical spirit is strong, latter-day reminders of the Sunday school in its heyday can be found.

The Sunday school at its height was the symbol of the most enduring religious movement in American history. It reached Americans of almost all classes, races and denominational affiliation for a dozen decades after the War of 1812–14. No other movement compares to it in appeal or cultural influence. In contrast, the civil rights crusade and the peace movement of the 1960s, or even the labor cause in the earlier years of the twentieth century, were comparatively short-lived, ephemeral eruptions. The astonishing durability of the Sunday school movement was not an accident. In the luxury of retrospect, a variety of reasons for its success can be discerned.

Success as a Movement

1. This movement survived, first of all, because of its capacity to maintain unity, even when it changed and despite enormous pressures toward diversity. Unlike the civil rights movement which, after two or three years of modest euphoria floundered on the question of class differences, the Sunday school retained its sense of solidarity for well over a century. How was this movement pyschology sustained? Through two devices: the uniform lesson plan and the convention system.

Though criticized and discredited for decades, the uniform lessons, or International Plan, represent a continuity that could persist into the future. Criticism of the plan has been plentiful and often valid but has usually missed the real point. Uniformity in lesson themes was an organizational device for maintaining unity among generations, denominations, and nations. (Evaluation of the new "Christian Education: Shared Approaches" curricula should not overlook the fact that these products of the ecumenical Joint Educational Development group utilize the uniform idea in some of its units. Supposed innovation frequently has precedent.)

Edward Eggleston, a Sunday school editor who wrote *The Hoosier Schoolmaster,* became one of the earliest and harshest critics of uniform lessons, although he had worked on a series that was a forerunner of the proposal approved at a national Sunday school convention in the early 1870s at the prompting of John H. Vincent and B. F. Jacobs. Remarked Eggleston, "Dr. Vincent and Mr. Jacobs will be able to look at a watch and tell a body just what identical printed questions they are reading simultaneously at [sic] little Baptist boys in Burmah, and little Methodist maids in Minnesota."[5] Vincent and Jacobs, for a matter of fact, were very much interested in just that possibility. Those "little Baptist boys" and "little Methodist maids" were doing something together, even if they were separated by geography, denomination, and culture. In "Burmah" and Minnesota, they were experiencing a ritualistic sign and seal of global unity. The uniform lesson system was intended as a declaration that nothing could tear the Sunday school movement apart—not denominational differences, not cleavages between nations or tensions among the races. Defenders of the plan embraced it as an emblem of a way of life, affirming their unity in spite of the odds against Protestants doing anything together for long. In an age desperately in need of symbols of unity the uniform lesson approach was reminder of a greater oneness that could transcend all differences.

The second device serving a passion for unity was the convention system. Following the Civil War, laymen such as Jacobs and a few ministers put together the intricate system that went a long way toward linking people from village, town, city, country, state, and nation—Canada and the United States—and the world. All this was accomplished in the early days without the help of a full-time staff. Each level in the system understood its responsibility. Local conventions, for example, focused on teacher training. Saturday afternoons in Buffalo, New York, in the late 1880s was a time when teachers, sometimes four or five hundred, met across denominational and congregational lines to engage in common preparation for the next day's Sunday school classes. The conventions helped to start new schools, to support schools in trouble and to inspire and train leaders. In those ways, they kept the movement together.

2. Another characteristic of a successful movement is the ability to create a liturgy of its own. Imbedded in that liturgy is the memory and the hope of a people—the past, present, and future celebrated in song and action. Chapter 3 details the Sunday school's special brand of music. The movement inspired song but was no less successful in institutionalizing liturgical action. There were, and in many congregations still are, the rituals of the weekly Sunday school assembly, the annual promotion day and picnic, and the distribution of pins or ribbons for perfect attendance. More spectacular (and less common today) were the Sunday school parades.

The *Penny Gazette* of 1855 described a western Sunday school celebration. According to the account, several Sunday schools in the "far-off borders of our land" combined to "unite and keep a holiday with pleasant and appropriate services and enjoyments as a means of social intercourse and improvement." The festivities took place in a clearing in the forest where some ox-drawn wagons carried a host of enthusiastic boosters. Each group had its own banner— "The Sunday School—the Hope of the World;" "We Won't Give Up the Bible"[6] (and who was asking them to give up the Bible?). Such occasions provided opportunity for a people to celebrate the convictions and hopes of a movement.

A mark of a successful movement related to liturgy is identification with a sacred cause. Without a sacred cause any movement will eventually disintegrate. The long life of the Sunday school movement was made possible, in large part, by its leaders' capacity to define a cause that was understandable to a wide range of persons of conflicting persuasions. Significantly, the cause presented an achievable goal yet suggested the mystery and romance of a great crusade. Early in the movement the most visible symbol of the cause were the poor children who needed schooling, manners, and religion. The Sunday school crusade really hit its stride in the 1820s and 1830s as it concentrated on preparing the way for conversion. That sense of purpose carried the movement well into the twentieth century (and still dominates vast numbers of Sunday schools.) The Sunday school has become so closely identified with conversion over the past 150 years that it is doubtful whether it could today be divorced from the evangelistic motivation. Certainly, none of the recently proposed substitutes— whether "character education" or "theological literacy" or "values training"—has ever quite replaced the evangelical concern for conversion as the movement's mainspring of energy.

The coming of the professional religious educators in the first two decades of the present century and the arrival of the church educational bureaucrats in the 1940s and 1950s did tend to undermine the Sunday school cause and its liturgy. Basic Protestant education is still trying to find its way through the maze created by the clash between the professionals and the old-time system of lay volunteers. And when it comes to success, the modern professionals have not—probably cannot—match that of either the American Sunday School Union or B. F. Jacobs and his "Illinois band."

3. Every movement finally rests upon a foundation of lay loyalty, and loyal laity the Sunday school enjoyed from its outset. The lay workers had a sense of ownership unexcelled in any other religious movement. They were

vigorously, self-consciously in control. Although anti-clericalism cropped up occasionally in the course of the nineteenth century, Sunday school enthusiasts were usually willing to include pastors in the enterprise so long as the clergy understood its place. Laymen held most top offices in the convention system, but it is important to note that the Sunday school movement always made room for the ministry of women. The woman of the early nineteenth century had suffered such social and religious repression that she was usually blocked from all formal participation in church life. She was allowed to pray silently and to sit in the congregation. Out of frustration with their lot and dedication to the Gospel, some women formed "female auxiliaries," the early forerunners of the woman's missionary and social organizations. Others worked in the Sunday school. The movement provided occasions for women to come together as a group and to take an active part in a common cause. Here, for the first time, women worked alongside men in church activities, spoke in Christian gatherings and at most of the conventions voted on issues before the delegates. It was in the Sunday school and the female auxiliaries that church women began to take timid steps toward equality with men in Protestant church life in the United States.

The laymen and laywomen of the nineteenth century Sunday school embodied the tradition of the amateur at its best. To speak of Sunday school workers as amateurs is not to depreciate them. One root meaning of "amateur" points toward caring and intelligent love. An amateur is not a person who does things poorly; rather, one who cares about an activity and is intelligent in the way in which he or she cares. The American Sunday school movement launched in the early nineteenth century cared about saving souls; its caring was passionate, sometimes overbearing, but not necessarily antiintellectual and seldom insensitive to individuals. From time to time the movement encouraged the development of intelligent mentors. For instance, John H. Vincent established a system of normal schools where Sunday school teachers would study the latest in pedagogy, Bible geography, and other relevant topics. He founded Chautauqua as a national Sunday school university and, eventually, from Chautauqua launched a nationwide system of local reading groups which encouraged adult education. The Chautauqua Literary and Scientific Circle sparked the first "book of the month" club, sending out volumes in response to the hunger for culture and religion among Sunday school teachers across the land.

What began and flourished as a movement of amateurs developed a remarkable capacity to balance the need for continuity and the imperative of change, a quality required of every successful movement. Movements that cannot change grind to a halt, or at least become fading cults of nostalgia. Movements that do not incarnate continuity with the past become so threatened by emerging forces that they tend to lose wide appeal and become sects. For a half century or more the leaders of the Sunday school managed to maintain stability while also encouraging innovation and change. The big little school appeared to be an integral part of a conservative social order. It appealed to frontier communities that welcomed Sunday school missionaries not so much because they were interested in Gospel offerings but because a Sunday school symbolized civic order and propriety. Succeeding generations of parents looked to the Sunday school as a way of taming their children and sustaining some link with the receding past. Yet the movement also harbored an interest in experimentation and encouraged change. Kindergartens, for example, were found in Sunday schools long before they entered the majority of the public school systems.

Sunday school workers in the late nineteenth century were among the pioneers in responding to the challenge of an emerging new stage of life—adolescence, a stage made possible as the young were allowed a childhood and a period of transition into adulthood. Some of the earliest efforts at formal adult education were begun under the auspices of the Sunday school.

Many of the contemporary problems of Protestant religious education, and of American Protestantism in general, arise from the loss of an ability to balance the need for continuity and the imperative of change. This, more than anything else, explains the chasms between conservatives and modernists, and too often precedents of balance are obscured as competing sides recast the past in the images of the present. Many evangelical and so-called "neo-evangelical" Protestants concerned with personal salvation do not know that revered predecessors, such as revivalist Charles G. Finney, were also ardent social reformers. Many activist Protestant liberals are ignorant of the evangelistic zeal of their heroes and heroines of yesteryear.

An American Ailment

The weaknesses of the Sunday school movement are no less interesting than its strengths and presumed virtues. Perhaps the deepest-set flaw was a congenital ailment that has afflicted most movements in the United States. This is a tendency to live off the mood of the moment, a characteristic that serious movements have willed to popular journalism and to the American advertising industry. Even at its best, the Sunday school movement was often living off the tides of the times. Its leaders seldom dipped below the surface of things to probe basic problems over an extended period. Instead, they were inclined to float from enthusiasm to enthusiasm as the way of keeping the movement going and its appeal growing. This tendency toward thinness of thought is especially evident in the Sunday school workers' preoccupation with technique.

In the earlier days, the Sunday school army was constantly engaged in trumpeting the values of procedures. Memorization was much in vogue in the early nineteenth century and that obsession produced several generations of virtuosi who could recount thousands of Bible verses, although without necessarily understanding the meaning of a single one. Sunday school curricula in the middle of the last century turned to biblical geography. Topographical maps of the Holy Land adorned classroom walls throughout the Protestant empire. At the turn of the century yet another technique had become prominent. This was the learning of Christian discipline through punctuality. The clock became a fixture in the Sunday school room, and there was a national organization called the "Old-Timer's Tribe" that had "a pledge to bind and a pin to remind." Other orders, such as the "Loyal Sunday School Army," also worked for punctuality and promptness. In Akron Plan Sunday school buildings, the clock was often well-placed; the superintendent's bell punctuated the orchestration of movements from one place to another, and the superintendent sat where he could watch the latecomers. Succeeding generations of Sunday school workers have been no less zealous in the pursuit of the newest in technique. For a century and a half the problem has been much the same: the presence of a popular procedure has allowed the absence of serious and critical reflection on technique to go unnoticed and unmourned.

A quality of thinness is evident elsewhere in the history of the Sunday school. It is apparent, for example, in the manner in which the movement avoided controversies that could have torn it apart. One of the divisive issues avoided

was, of course, race relations. This was true both before
and after the Civil War, and the Sunday school took no
leadership in the civil rights movement of the 1960s, at
least not in the white-dominated denominations or in the
ecumenical expressions of the enterprise.

Another major failure of the Sunday school is symbolized by the Bible. As long as the authority of the Scrip-
tures was not questioned, the Sunday school enjoyed the
full weight of "thus sayeth the Lord." Yet by the 1880s and
1890s the threat of biblical criticism was unavoidable. By
and large, the Sunday school simply failed to meet the
challenge of the higher critics. Despite a variety of valiant
efforts to popularize biblical scholarship and make its finding available to a mass following, the majority of Sunday
school leaders managed to ignore this threat, to keep
going as though the biblical critics had never written a
single word. To this day, the average Sunday school has
not been able to mediate the difference between the teachings of the best of the scriptural experts and the opinions
of rank-and-file church members. It was not a bit surprising when in 1979 the nation's best-known Sunday school
teacher, President Jimmy Carter, indicated his almost
complete ignorance of higher biblical criticism. In some
respects, it is little wonder that the disdainful phrase, "a
Sunday school faith," has come to be synonymous with
superficiality and self-protective innocence. Perhaps this
penchant for thinness is the most legitimate reason why
American historians and theologians have overlooked the
big little school.

A Third Century

The laymen who reorganized the Sunday school after
the Civil War had no doubts that they were involved in a

sacred cause that would endure time. John H. Vincent declared: "In the interest of the church, the home, the state and society, we who represent the Sunday school say with Robert Browning our song of hope:

> 'the best is yet to be, the last
> for which the first was made.'"[7]

A century later it is not possible to affirm that for the Sunday school "the best is yet to be." In all likelihood, the best has been. The Protestant religious and educational ecology that produced the Sunday school has been ravaged almost to the point of obliteration as a national and international force. American Protestantism is divided on the value and necessity of the institution.

The Sunday school movement could probably never happen again. No large scale movement can develop today in the same way that the nineteenth century ones took hold and extended their lives over decades. A media society such as America has used up movements as fodder for the news and the commercialization of trends. A new Sunday school movement would not have time to germinate, to grow and make its mistakes without the hot glare of publicity exposing it to a society that, quickly bored, seeks new sensations. In this respect, the Sunday school may qualify as the last great religious movement in America. Its longevity and vigor has assuredly outdistanced the other nineteenth-century movements sired by the Revival.

But to say that no new Sunday school movement could happen is not to read an obituary, although as an institution the big little school is in disarray. The old movement and its spin-offs live; therefore, consideration of Sunday school's third century is in order.

For the immediate future, the Sunday school shows

every indication that it will just keep rolling along, the momentum catching up both the professionals and the old-timers. It continues as an enterprise of considerable magnitude and complexity, involving some 40 to 45 million persons in North America. Among the more conservative evangelicals, membership is growing, at least pulling out of the early 1970s leveling that some see as caused by excessive professionalism. Mainline enrollment declines, sometimes in spite of sophisticated revitalization plans designed by professionals desperate to enliven a volunteer movement. Some denominations are not far from throwing in the towel, which is virtually what the United Church of Canada has done. With a decrease of over 400,000 from 1971 to 1976, the Canadians have, by and large, decided not to tax themselves by the search for reforms to rebuild the "big little school." Their hope is for some other type of educational method.

Today in the United States schools are of every possible size and outlook. Observers on any Sunday morning could visit church classrooms embodying a different stage of the movement's development. A fair number have incorporated the spirit of the neo-orthodox *church school* of the 1950s. Avant-garde centers exist and their experimentation represents a revival of the *progressive school* in religious education. And the "Middletown" *Sunday school* proliferates. The largest across the decade of the 1970s were latter-day versions of John Wanamaker's Bethany school a hundred years earlier. According to a sympathetic observer, the secret of present success is "the energetic minister who leads his flock like a president runs a corporation."[8] This clerical leadership runs counter to the old Sunday school model of lay domination, but, minus the clerical slant, Wanamaker advocated almost the same thing.

Curricular materials are constantly undergoing change as the Sunday school moves into its third century. Literature from the more conservative, often independent, publishers may be as conversion-conscious as the books issued by the American Sunday School Union, but they are more colorful and more sensitive to the pyschology of learning along the age spectrum. The denominational educational agencies and their ecumenical consortia dabble with combinations of the new and the old, their basic dilemma being the question of how to make a cafeteria approach to materials—and thereby satisfy a pluralistic constituency—economically viable. While the denominational publishers on the mainline generally want to keep up with the best in American education, they are also driven by what sociologist Peter Berger calls the "logic of market economics." In pluralistic societies, Berger notes, religious institutions may not take for granted the allegiance of members. The tradition, once imposed by authoritative means, must be sold—"the religious institutions become marketing agencies and the religious traditions become consumer commodities."⁹ This sales task becomes all the harder when a denomination is no longer quite sure what its tradition is and whether it approves of what it thinks the tradition may be. Still, the proliferation of materials offered gives odds in favor of some superior literature. Whether it is properly used or not is another matter.

Despite more and better material the classroom scene in most Sunday schools is approximately what it was fifty to sixty years ago. The failure of the professional church educator to revolutionize popular custom was to be expected. Typical teachers today receive about as little help and training as did their grandmothers, which is much less than was the case in the heyday of uniform lessons. Most ministers remain indifferent to Sunday school affairs unless some unusual trouble arises. A study in the mid-decades of the twentieth century indicated that pastors spent less than 5 percent of their time on the educational work of the church, or "little more than they have to give to janitorial services."[10] Aside from the fact that it is a rare pastor who wields a broom in the 1980s, the data is probably still reliable. Scores upon scores of Sunday schools in urban and rural areas function, as they always have, in relative separation from the rest of the church. "Sunday school is Sunday school" and "church is church," and in western Nebraska and on Tennessee's Cumberland Plateau one can skip the latter but not the former if social respectability is to be maintained. (The same separation exists in Boston, The Bronx, and suburban Los Angeles, only there one can skip Sunday school and church in perpetuity with no loss of social standing.) Given the tensions that have existed between Sunday school and congregation, superintendent, and pastor, it is somewhat amazing that the educational program has survived at all.

Consciously or unconsciously, virtually all denominations in the United States are observing the bicentennial of Robert Raikes' "charity" school by pondering ways in which the Sunday schools can be reformed or adapted to better serve the goal of religious instruction. Among the churches, the historic black communions face special challenges introduced by their experiences in the 1960s, particularly the black power movement. Following a natural impulse, the black denominations long ago moved toward the preparation of educational material appropriate to the black struggle for freedom and justice. This process was speeded up in the 1960s and, as stated earlier, many black educators within the church saw the Sunday school as the logical place to introduce youths to the newer versions of black liberation theology. At the same time, the liberation forces within black Christianity tended to lump the Sunday school with a kind of religion seen as teaching subservient attitudes.

Black churches, no longer needed to provide literacy, are probably harder pressed than their white counterparts to define the role of Sunday training. In fact, reports from both east and west coasts (Baltimore and the Los Angeles area) indicate that some black churches are abandoning schools on Sunday in favor of Saturday programs broader in cultural scope than the old classes. For example, Baltimore's New Shiloah Baptist Church had a dying Sunday school of about a hundred members in 1973 when it decided to switch to a Saturday morning program. Within five years, 450 persons ranging in age from eight to seventy-five were enrolled.[11] The idea of Saturday school encompassing religion, ethnic concerns, and some remedial education seems to have been pioneered in Los Angeles by eight congregations who joined an ecumenical educational growth organization.[12]

In some estimations the black church lost ground in the black community during the period of black power militancy, yet the erosion of loyalty was not as widespread as the strongest critics of black Christianity anticipated. The denominations were able to absorb much of the criticism directed at them from within and from outside. They benefitted at times by listening to their critics, and they generally emerged from the 1960s with a strong sense of their responsibility in the educating of whole persons. Many black congregations do not appear to be as locked into inherited forms of education as their white counterparts. Technique is less important than the goal. "Black religious education among Afro-americans ought to produce more joyful sons and daughters of God!"[13] according to Calvin E. Bruce. Omit the word "black" and substitute any ethnic grouping, or just "Christian," for "Afro-american," and Bruce's statement is a worthy objective for all Christian education, and for the Sunday school in its third century.

An Unfinished Enterprise

The two-hundredth anniversary of the Sunday school is no occasion for drawing conclusions about the movement in America because the story is unfinished. The big little school deserves more attention as historical and present phenomenon than it has received from scholars, but any who approach it must be willing to leave blank pages at the end of their work.

It is already clear that three popular attitudes toward the Sunday school since the 1950s are each off base. The positive attitude was summed up by J. Edgar Hoover who, as a former superintendent, praised the Sunday school as a "crime prevention laboratory."[14] The negative was put forth in a *Life* magazine article that said the Sunday school is sometimes "the most wasted hour of the week."[15] The third is simple disregard. All three are wrong because they are simplistic. The crime problem is more complicated than Hoover implied, or possibly could comprehend; the *Life* comment is an extravagant vote of confidence in how people spend the rest of their time; and the option of disregard misses a huge segment of Americans who are just being Americans.

From the vantage point of the Time-Life building or the lofty professionalism of seminaries, it has been easy to overlook the Sunday school as the incarnation of popular Protestantism. The big little school has given and continues to give millions of youngsters some sense of how Protestants think, feel, act, and sing. For people who have painfully discarded much of their heritage to accommodate pluralism, it is a rare "immemorial custom." In spite of all the negative evaluations of sophisticated culture, the Sunday school may add up to an educational alternative more humane than public or private institutions that have responded to industrial society's insatiable desire for more technologists and bureaucrats. Restless students have hardly asked for the tutelage of little misses doing their duty on Sunday, but they are often searching for something akin to what the Sunday school offers. They want to know what life does, or might, mean. No one should overlook the fact that evangelical, even fundamentalist, congregations that still use the Sunday school as a forum for conversion are not the ones lacking teenagers in their pews. Mainline congregations that view Sunday school as a place to learn *about* religion, in case a person should ever become religious, are the ones with fewer youth groups. Many of their children, like those of many a secular family, have fled to strange cults, or to the evangelical churches.

The Sunday school at its best has tried to illumine Protestantism's answers to the questions of the meaning of life. It has talked about life and death, hope and love, faith and forgiveness. The big little school has concentrated time and attention on matters, such as the geography of the Holy Land, marginal to the questions of meaning. But knowing the road from Damascus to Jerusalem prior to entering the chaotic maze of modern ideologies may prepare a mind to deal with the traumas that threaten each person in the closing decades of the twentieth century. The possibility is worth considering.

Not so long ago in the modern technological age author Willie Morris went to a Methodist Sunday school in the deep South. He recalls that

... Our teacher told us stories about the Bible, or helped us make religious posters, or led us in singing: Jesus loves me! this I

know. . . . Later as we grew older there would be more sophisticated Sunday School sessions, when we would sit in small circles
and talk about religion and how we could get the children who
had not showed up that Sunday more interested in it. We would
hold hands and pray, and whisper the benediction, and dream
up projects to make our class the most attractive in the whole
church and how best to help out the preacher in his many duties.
We would read Bible verses and discuss their hidden meaning.[16]

That is how it was around 1880, too, and how it is still in
many, many white and black Methodist and Baptist
churches—even in the Riverdale Presbyterian Church, an
ethnically mixed congregation in one of New York City's
most affluent neighborhoods. It may not be that way in
another century, and yet the big little school may still be
around. Minds change slowly in that still forceful middle-
class Protestant culture which largely shaped the United
States. Those Protestant goals of prosperity and future
blessedness—and sometimes purity—long ago became the
aims of Americans of all races and religions.

The Sunday school is one of the major continuities making America what it is and upholding the dreams of what it
wants to become at its best. As a movement it has survived
too long, exerted too much influence to be dismissed in the
study of the past or in anticipation of the future. At least
among enthusiastic evangelicals, who form a large segment of American Protestantism, the Sunday school re-
tains the qualities F. D. Huntington saw in it more than a
century ago:

The Sunday school appears to take on the character of an endless
experiment by the grandeur of its objective, by the inexhaustible
interest it touches, by the immortality of the soul it nourishes,
as well as by the variety of the conditions in which it exists. It is
invested with this mystery and charm of an unfinished enterprise. Its plan is never quite filled out.[17]

Notes

1. John Westerhoff, "A Future for the Sunday School," *The Duke Divinity School Review* (XL, Fall, 1975), p. 194.
2. Martin E. Marty, "American Sunday School May be Defunct," *Context* (May 1, 1975), p. 2.
3. *World-Wide Sunday School Work*, ed. William N. Hartshorn (Chicago: World's Sunday School Association, 1910), p. 47.
4. Cited by Edward Eggleston, "Unpopular Words," *Sunday School Time* (XVIII, May 20, 1876), p. 321.
5. Ibid., p. 191.
6. "A Western Sunday School Celebration," *Penny Gazette* (XIII, no. 5, 1855), p. 1.
7. John H. Vincent, *Modern Sunday School* (New York: Hunt and Eaton, 1887), p. 164.
8. Elmer Towns, "America's Largest Sunday Schools," *Christian Life* (XXXII, August, 1970), p. 16-17.
9. Peter Berger, *The Sacred Canopy* (Garden City: Doubleday & Company, Inc., 1967), p. 137.
10. Cited by J. Paul Williams, "When the Clergy Abdicates,"*The Christian Century* (LXIII, January 16, 1946), p. 74.
11. Reported by Religious News Service, March 23, 1978.
12. John Hurst Adams, "Saturday Ethnic School: A Model," *Spectrum, International Journal of Religious Education* (XLIV, July–August, 1971), pp. 8-9, 32.
13. Calvin E. Bruce, "Refocusing Black Religious Education: Three Imperatives," *Religious Education* (LXIX, July–August, 1974), p., 432.
14. Edward L. R. Elson, "J. Edgar Hoover—Churchman," *Presbyterian Life* (I, November 27, 1948), p. 5.
15. Wesley Shrader, "Our Troubled Sunday Schools," *Life* (XLII, February 11, 1957), p. 110.
16. Willie Morris, *North Toward Home* (Boston: Houghton Mifflin Company, 1967), p. 40.
17. F. D. Huntington, *The Relation of the Sunday School to the Church* (Boston: Henry Hoyt, 1860), pp. 3–4.

Acknowledgments

This volume grew out of a study project on "The History of the World Sunday School Movement," and would not have been possible apart from the imaginative foresight and generosity of several interested friends of the former World Council of Christian Education(WCCE), now integrated into the World Council of Churches. In particular, we would like to pay tribute to Mr. Coleman Burke for his leadership, as well as to Dr. Ralph N. Mould. Mr. Loren Walters and the New York Office of the WCCE also assisted our work in various ways. Although the Council was cooperative from the outset, neither it nor its successor agency should be held responsible for any of the particular judgments expressed in this book.

We are likewise grateful to Dr. William B. Kennedy, formerly of the World Council of Churches and now at Union Theological Seminary, New York, who, together with Professor Robert T. Handy of Union encouraged us not to be satisfied with safe or easy answers to complex problems of historical interpretation. We were also greatly helped by the advice of Dr. C. Ellis Nelson, now president of Louisville Presbyterian Theological Seminary. Dr. Gerald E. Knoff of New York graciously shared his insights. So did one of the venerable scholars of the Sunday school—Dr. Luther A. Weigle, whose contributions to the movement have been immeasurable.

We also wish to acknowledge the *Duke Divinity School Review* in which an earlier version of part of the last chapter of the present volume appeared (Volume 40, Fall, 1975).

We owe much to the findings and speculations of our associates in research, men and women first known as students but who have since the first edition of this book taken their places as professors or other leaders in church and society: Robert Craig, who assisted in the whole enterprise; James Fraser, who investigated the beginnings of the American Sunday school; Robert Harsh, who gave help all along the way; Alice Dickerson Hatt, who led us all in the rediscovery of the musical heritage of the Sunday school; and not least, Emily Hewitt, whose explorations of the nineteenth-century literature were valuable and instructive. Professor Grant S. Shockley of Emory University took time to develop the outlines of a history of the black Sunday school in America. Professor Charles Kniker of Iowa State University located some material crucial for our narrative.

Our appreciation to Lillian Block, editor-in-chief of Religious News Service, who opened the files of her organization to us for both the first and second editions of this book. We are most grateful to associates, critics and friends who responded warmly to our work when it first appeared in 1971.

We owe great thanks to Dr. Blaine Fister of the National Council of Churches who proposed a second edition to coincide with the bicentennial of the Sunday school, and to Dr. James Michael Lee of Religious Education Press for readily agreeing to publish this new revised and enlarged edition.

The authors recall with special appreciation the spirited help of numerous persons during the hectic months of writing a small book about a large topic: the encouragement of our wives, Katharine Lynn and Juanita Wright; the aid of Mrs. Jean Stetson of North Leeds, Maine; the support of staff members of Auburn Theological Seminary—Mrs. Rosalee Maxwell and Mrs. Shirley Skirvin, and particularly the editorial work of Mrs. Virginia Clifford.

Index of Names

Index of Subjects